The Bubble of
American Supremacy

The Bubble of American Supremacy

CORRECTING THE MISUSE
OF AMERICAN POWER

GEORGE SOROS

Weidenfeld & Nicolson

LONDON

First published in Great Britain in 2004
by Weidenfeld & Nicolson

The Orion Publishing Group Ltd
Orion House
5 Upper St Martin's Lane
London WC2H 9EA

Fourth impression 2004

Originally published in the United States by PublicAffairs
A member of the Perseus Books Group

A CIP catalogue record for this book is
available from the British Library.

ISBN: 0 297 84906 9

Printed in Great Britain by
Clays Ltd, St Ives plc

Contents

Preface

I consider the Bush doctrine of preemptive military action pernicious, and so do many others around the world. The invasion of Iraq was the first practical application of the Bush doctrine, and it elicited an allergic reaction worldwide—not because anyone had a good word to say about Saddam Hussein, but because we insisted on invading Iraq unilaterally without any clear evidence that he had anything to do with September 11 or that he possessed weapons of mass destruction.

The gap in perceptions between America and the rest of the world has never been wider. Abroad, America is seen as abusing the dominant position it occupies; public opinion at home has been led to believe that Saddam Hussein posed a clear and present danger to our national security. Only in the aftermath of the Iraqi invasion are people becoming aware that they have been misled.

I contend that the Bush administration has deliberately exploited September 11 in order to pursue policies that the American public would not have otherwise tolerated. The Bush dream of American supremacy is both unattainable and in contradiction with the principles that America has traditionally stood for. It endangers our values as well as our security. And it endangers the world because America is so powerful.

Preface

The United States enjoys a dominant position in the world today that cannot be challenged by any other state or combination of states for the foreseeable future. It can lose its dominance only as a result of its own mistakes. At present the country is in the process of committing such mistakes because it is in the hands of a group of extremists whose strong sense of mission is matched only by their false sense of certitude. By abusing the position that the United States occupies in the world, the extremists have made our nation weaker, not stronger.

These are fighting words and many people will violently disagree, but they are justified by the gravity of the situation. These are not normal times. I have made it my primary objective to persuade the American public to reject President Bush in the forthcoming elections. We have been deceived. When he stood for election in 2000, President Bush promised a humble foreign policy, not the Bush doctrine. If he is rejected in 2004, his policies can be written off as a temporary aberration and America can resume its rightful place in the world. On the other hand, if he is reelected, the electorate will have endorsed those policies and we will have to live with the consequences. But it is not enough to defeat President Bush at the polls. America has to reexamine its role in the world and adopt a more constructive vision.

·   ·   ·

My own sensitivity to the excesses of the Bush administration may be attributed in large part to my background. I grew up as a Jew in Hungary during World War II. I lived through both German and Soviet occupation and learned at an early age how political systems can affect your very survival. When I hear President Bush say that "either you are with us, or you are with the terrorists," I hear alarm bells.* John Ashcroft pushes the wrong buttons in me when he declares, "To those who scare peace-loving people with phantoms of lost liberty, my message is this: Your tactics only aid terrorists, for they erode our national unity and diminish our resolve. They give ammunition to America's enemies and pause to America's friends."† I am distressed that the public is not as alarmed as I am. This is not the America I chose as my home.

When I escaped from Hungary in 1947, I first went to England and studied at the London School of Economics. I came under the influence of Karl Popper the philosopher and learned about the difference between open and closed societies. After I had been successful in the financial markets, I established a network of foundations fostering open societies. As a practical promoter of democracy in various parts of the world, I feel qualified to contribute to a rethinking of America's role in the world.

I bring to the task a conceptual framework that I started

---

*George W. Bush, Address to a Joint Session of Congress and the American People, September 20, 2001, available at http://www.whitehouse.gov/news/releases/2001/09/20010920–8.html.
†John Ashcroft, Testimony to Senate Committee on the Judiciary, December 6, 2001, available at http://www.usdoj.gov/ag/testimony/2001/1206transcriptsenatejudiciarycommittee.htm.

developing in my student days and kept revising in the light of experience. In many ways it differs from the prevailing wisdom. Some of the terms I use—open society, reflexivity, radical fallibility, fertile fallacies, the human uncertainty principle, and the various stages of the boom-bust process—may be unfamiliar to the reader. I give a brief explanation of my conceptual framework in the Appendix.

.   .   .

This book has grown out of my previous one: *George Soros on Globalization.** In that book, I examined our international financial and trade institutions (IFTIs) and suggested ways to make them more effective. At that time, my main concern was with the excesses of market fundamentalists who are opposed to any interference with market forces. They attacked our IFTIs from the right while the antiglobalization movement was assailing those institutions from the left. I recognized the deficiencies of the global capitalist system, and I argued that they could be cured by reforming and strengthening our IFTIs, not by destroying them. Of course, my argument was at odds with the Bush administration's posture, but September 11 gave rise to a moment of national reflection that might have led to a change of attitudes, and I did not want to let the moment pass.

President Bush led the country—and the world—in a different direction. He used September 11 to assert our right to

*New York: PublicAffairs, 2002.

preemptive military action. My main concern now is with the excesses of that approach. The government of the most powerful country on earth has fallen into the hands of extremists who are guided by a crude form of social Darwinism: Life is a struggle for survival, and we must rely mainly on the use of force to survive. This is a distorted view: The survival of the fittest depends on cooperation as well as competition. The pursuit of military superiority is closely allied with market fundamentalism, which also emphasizes competition to the detriment of cooperation. But the Bush administration was able to carry the nation behind it by playing up the terrorist threat.

Prior to September 11, the excesses of a false ideology were kept within bounds by the normal functioning of our democracy. The war on terror temporarily silenced criticism and carried us beyond normalcy. It is when we invaded Iraq that we entered what I call far-from-equilibrium territory. I see a certain parallel between the pursuit of American supremacy and the boom-bust pattern that can be observed from time to time in the stock market. The bubble is now bursting. The purpose of this book is to explain how we got into the mess in which we currently find ourselves and what America's role in the world ought to be. I shall subject the Bush administration's policies to critical examination in Part 1 and spell out a constructive vision of America's role in Part 2.

Acknowledgments

This book has been published at great speed because of the urgency of the subject. I would like to thank the editors of the *Atlantic Monthly* who saw its importance and gave it early support by agreeing to take an excerpt.

Several people read the manuscript at various stages of its evolution and contributed to a spirited debate that enriched the conclusions reached here. Although there were fewer advance readers than usual because of the pressures of time, I'm indebted especially to them, notably: Benjamin Barber, Emma Bonino, Robert Boorstin, Leon Botstein, Yehuda Elkana, Mort Halperin, Karin Lissakers, William Maynes, Bill Moyers, Wiktor Osiatynski, Paul Soros, Michael Vachon, Byron Wien, and Fareed Zakaria. David Stevens assisted me with research. Yvonne Sheer did much more than type and retype the manuscript innumerable times; she did a lot of research and coordinated the entire effort. At, PublicAffairs, Peter Osnos, Robert Kimzey, Clive Priddle, Melanie Peirson Johnstone, Jenny Dossin, and Patricia Boyd went to great lengths to get the book done and arrange for the timely publication of the extract. It has been a pleasure to work with the team again.

To all I am truly grateful.

GEORGE SOROS

October 2003

PART **I**

A Critical View

CHAPTER 1

The Bush Doctrine

It is generally agreed that September 11, 2001, changed the course of history, but we must ask ourselves why that should be so. How could a single event, even if it involved three thousand civilian casualties, have such a far-reaching effect? The answer lies not so much in the event itself but in the way the United States, under the leadership of President George W. Bush, responded to it.

Admittedly, the terrorist attack was a historic event in its own right. Hijacking fully loaded airplanes and using them as suicide bombs was an audacious idea, and the execution could not have been more spectacular. The destruction of the twin towers of the World Trade Center made a symbolic statement that reverberated around the world, and the fact that people could watch the event on their television sets endowed it with an emotional impact that no terrorist act had ever achieved before.

The aim of terrorism is by definition to terrorize, and the attack of September 11 fully accomplished this objective. Most people in America were shaken to their core. They were affected both individually and collectively. Until then, the idea that the United States could be challenged on its own soil and that U.S. citizens may be personally vulnerable did not enter into Americans' consciousness. The attack shattered people's sense of security. A feeling of normalcy was replaced by a sense of emergency.

Even so, September 11, 2001, could not have changed the course of history to the extent that it has if President Bush had not responded to it the way he did. He declared war on terrorism and under that guise implemented a radical foreign policy agenda that predated the tragedy of September 11.

The underlying principles of this agenda can be summed up as follows: International relations are relations of power, not law; power prevails and law legitimizes what prevails. The United States is unquestionably the dominant power in the post–Cold War world; it is therefore in a position to impose its views, interests, and values on the world. The world would benefit from adopting American values because the American model has demonstrated its superiority. Under the previous administrations, however, the United States failed to use the full potential of its power. This has to be corrected. The United States must assert its supremacy in the world.

This view on foreign policy is part of a comprehensive ideology customarily referred to as neoconservatism, but I prefer to describe it as a crude form of social Darwinism. I call it crude because it ignores the role of cooperation in the survival of the fittest and puts all the emphasis on competition. In the economy, the competition is between firms; in international relations, it is between states. In economic matters, social Darwinism takes the form of market fundamentalism; in international relations, it leads to the pursuit of American supremacy.

Not all the members of the Bush administration subscribe to this ideology, but the neocons form an influential group within the executive branch and their influence greatly increased after September 11. Their ideas were succinctly stated in the 1997 mission statement of the Project for the New American Century, a neoconservative think tank and policy advocacy group. Already in 1992, under the first Bush administration, a similar memorandum had been prepared by the Defense Department, but it proved so controversial that it had to be dropped. It is worth quoting the 1997 mission statement and its signatories in full:*

*Project for the New American Century, Statement of Principles, June 3, 1997, Project for the New American Century Web site, http://www.newamericancen tury.org.

STATEMENT OF PRINCIPLES

American foreign and defense policy is adrift. Conservatives have criticized the incoherent policies of the Clinton Administration. They have also resisted isolationist impulses from within their own ranks. But conservatives have not confidently advanced a strategic vision of America's role in the world. They have not set forth guiding principles for American foreign policy. They have allowed differences over tactics to obscure potential agreement on strategic objectives. And they have not fought for a defense budget that would maintain American security and advance American interests in the new century.

We aim to change this. We aim to make the case and rally support for American global leadership.

As the 20th century draws to a close, the United States stands as the world's preeminent power. Having led the West to victory in the Cold War, America faces an opportunity and a challenge: Does the United States have the vision to build upon the achievements of past decades? Does the United States have the resolve to shape a new century favorable to American principles and interests?

We are in danger of squandering the opportunity and failing the challenge. We are living off the capital—both the military investments and the foreign policy achievements—built up by past administrations. Cuts in foreign affairs and defense spending, inattention to the tools of statecraft, and inconstant leadership are making it increasingly difficult to sustain American influence around the world. And the promise of short-term commercial benefits threatens to override strategic considerations. As a consequence, we are jeopardizing the nation's ability to meet present threats and to deal with potentially greater challenges that lie ahead.

We seem to have forgotten the essential elements of the Reagan Administration's success: a military that is strong and ready to meet both present and future challenges; a foreign policy that boldly and purposefully promotes American principles abroad; and national leadership that accepts the United States' global responsibilities.

Of course, the United States must be prudent in how it exercises its power. But we cannot safely avoid the responsibilities of global leadership or the costs that are associated with its exercise. America has a vital role in maintaining peace and security in Europe, Asia, and the Middle East. If we shirk our responsibilities, we invite challenges to our fundamental interests. The history of the 20th century should have taught us that it is important to shape circumstances before crises emerge, and to meet threats before they become dire. The history of this century should have taught us to embrace the cause of American leadership.

Our aim is to remind Americans of these lessons and to draw their consequences for today. Here are four consequences:

- we need to increase defense spending significantly if we are to carry out our global responsibilities today and modernize our armed forces for the future;

- we need to strengthen our ties to democratic allies and to challenge regimes hostile to our interests and values;

- we need to promote the cause of political and economic freedom abroad;

- we need to accept responsibility for America's unique role in preserving and extending an international order friendly to our security, our prosperity, and our principles.

Such a Reaganite policy of military strength and moral clarity may not be fashionable today. But it is necessary if the United States is to build on the successes of this past century and to ensure our security and our greatness in the next.

Elliott Abrams	Steve Forbes	Dan Quayle
Gary Bauer	Aaron Friedberg	Peter W. Rodman
William J. Bennett	Francis Fukuyama	Stephen P. Rosen
Jeb Bush	Frank Gaffney	Henry S. Rowen
Dick Cheney	Fred C. Ikle	Donald Rumsfeld
Eliot A. Cohen	Donald Kagan	Vin Weber
Midge Decter	Zalmay Khalilzad	George Weigel
Paula Dobriansky	I. Lewis Libby	Paul Wolfowitz
	Norman Podhoretz	

In 1998, many of the same signatories sent to President Clinton an open letter in which they argued for the invasion of Iraq. Five years later, they were in charge of the invasion, Dick Cheney as vice president, Donald Rumsfeld as secretary of defense, Paul Wolfowitz as his deputy, Zalmay Khalilzad as the envoy of the Pentagon, and the others as advocates and ideologues both inside and outside the government.* These people had a clear idea of the direction in which they wanted to take the country, and when

*Elliott Abrams is senior director for Near East and North African affairs, National Security Council; Gary Bauer was a presidential contender in 2000 and is president of American Values; William J. Bennett is a conservative commentator and a Distinguished Fellow at the Heritage Foundation; Jeb Bush is governor of Florida; Eliot Cohen is a professor of strategic studies at Johns Hopkins University, School of Advanced International Studies, and a member of the Defense Policy Board at the Department of Defense; Midge Decter is a conservative commentator and author of a recent biography of Donald Rumsfeld; Paula Dobriansky is undersecretary for global affairs at the Department of State; Steve Forbes was a presidential contender in 2000 and is president and CEO of Forbes; Aaron Friedberg is a professor of politics and international affairs at Princeton University; Francis Fukuyama is a professor of international political economy at Johns Hopkins University, School of Advanced International Studies, and a member of the President's Council on Bioethics; Frank Gaffney is president of the Center for Security Policy; Fred Ikle is a Distinguished Scholar at the Center for Strategic and International Studies and a member of the Defense Policy Board at the Department of Defense; Donald Kagan is a professor of history and classics at Yale University; Lewis Libby is Dick Cheney's chief of staff; Norman Podhoretz is a Senior Fellow at the Hudson Institute and editor at large for *Commentary*; Dan Quayle is a former vice president and a member of the Defense Policy Board at the Department of Defense; Peter Rodman is assistant secretary of defense for International Security Affairs; Stephen Rosen is a professor of national security and military affairs at Harvard University; Henry Rowen is a Senior Fellow at the Hoover Institution and a member of the Defense Policy Board at the Department of Defense; Vin Weber is a partner at Clark and Weinstock (management consulting firm); George Weigel is a Senior Fellow at the Ethics and Public Policy Center.

the September 11 terrorist attacks presented an opportunity, they seized it without ever coming clean about all of their goals. The public is still not fully aware of this history.

Prior to September 11, 2001, the ideologues of the Project for the New American Century were hindered in implementing their strategy by two considerations. First, President Bush came to office without a clear mandate—he was elected president by a single vote on the Supreme Court. Second, America did not have a clearly defined enemy that would have justified a dramatic increase in military spending. The strategy advocated prior to September 11 was not identical with the one adopted afterward—it emphasized missile defense rather than the war on terrorism—but it was infused with the same spirit of seeking unilateral American dominance.

September 11 removed both obstacles in one stroke. President Bush declared war on terrorism, and the nation lined up behind its president. Then the Bush administration proceeded to exploit the terrorist attack for its own purposes. To silence criticism and keep the nation united behind the president, the administration deliberately fostered the fear that has gripped the country. It then used the war on terrorism to pursue its dream of American supremacy. That is how September 11 changed the course of history.

Exploiting an event to further an agenda is not inherently reprehensible. It is the task of the president to provide leadership, and it is only natural for politicians to twist, exploit, or manipulate events to promote their policies. The cause for concern is to be found in the policies that President Bush is promoting and in the way he is going about imposing them. President Bush is leading the United States and the world in a very dangerous direction.

SUPREMACIST IDEOLOGY

The supremacist ideology of the Bush administration is in contradiction with the principles of an open society because it claims possession of an ultimate truth. It postulates that because we are stronger than others, we must know better and we must have right on our side. That is where religious fundamentalism comes together with market fundamentalism to form the ideology of American supremacy. The very first sentence of our latest national security strategy reads as follows: "The great struggles of the twentieth century between liberty and totalitarianism ended with a decisive victory for the forces of freedom— and a single sustainable model for national success: freedom, democracy, and free enterprise."

This statement is false on two counts. First, there is no single, sustainable model for national success. And second, the American model, which has been successful, is not available to others, because our success depends greatly on our dominant position at the center of the global capitalist system and we are not willing to yield this position to others.

The Bush doctrine, first enunciated in the president's speech at West Point in June 2002 and then incorporated in the national security strategy in September 2002, is built on two pillars: First, the United States will do everything in its power to maintain its unquestioned military supremacy and, second, the United States arrogates the right to preemptive action. Taken together, these two pillars support two classes of sovereignty: the sovereignty of the United States, which takes precedence over international treaties and obligations, and the sovereignty of all other states, which is subject to the Bush doctrine. This is reminiscent of George Orwell's *Animal Farm*: All animals are equal, but some animals are more equal than others.

To be sure, the Bush doctrine is not stated so starkly; it is buried in Orwellian doublespeak. The doublespeak is needed because of the contradiction between the Bush administration's concept of freedom and democracy and the actual principles of freedom and democracy. Talk of spreading democracy looms large in the national security strategy. When President Bush says, as he does frequently, that "freedom" will prevail, in fact he means that America will prevail. I am rather sensitive to Orwellian doublespeak because I grew up with it in Hungary first under Nazi and later Communist rule.

In his address to Congress nine days after the terrorist attacks of September 11, President Bush declared, "The advance of human freedom—the great achievement of our time, and the great hope of our time—now depends on us. Our nation—this generation—will lift a dark threat of violence from our people and our future. We will rally the world to this cause by our efforts, by our courage."* In a free and open society, however, people are supposed to decide for themselves what they mean by freedom and democracy and not simply follow America's lead.

The contradiction has been brought home by the current occupation of Iraq. We came as liberators bringing "freedom and democracy," but that is not how we are perceived by a large part of the population. The military part of the campaign went better than could have been expected, but the occupation turned into a disaster.

The dearth of thought given to, and preparation for, the aftermath of the invasion is truly amazing, especially when so many critics had been so vocal in warning about the difficulties. It can be explained only by a confusion in the mind of President Bush, which has been exploited by the advocates of the Iraqi invasion. President Bush equates freedom with American values. He has a simplistic view of what is right and what is wrong: *We* are right and *they* are wrong. This is in

*George W. Bush, address to a joint session of Congress and the American people, U.S. Capitol, Washington, D.C., September 20, 2001, available at www.whitehouse.gov/news/releases/2001/09/20010920–8.html.

contradiction with the principles of open society, which recognize that *we* may be wrong.

It is ironic that the government of the most successful open society in the world should have fallen into the hands of ideologues who ignore the first principles of open society. Who would have thought sixty years ago, when Karl Popper wrote *Open Society and Its Enemies*, that the United States itself could pose a threat to open society? Yet that is what is happening, both internally and internationally. At home, Attorney General John Ashcroft has used the war on terrorism to curtail civil liberties. Abroad, the United States is trying to impose its views and interests on the rest of the world by the use of military force, and it has proclaimed its right to do so in the Bush doctrine.

The invasion of Iraq was the first practical application of the Bush doctrine, and it turned out to be counterproductive. A chasm has opened between America and the rest of the world. That is what Osama Bin Laden must have been hoping for. By declaring war on terrorism and invading Iraq, President Bush has played right into the terrorists' hands.

DISCONTINUITY

September 11 introduced a discontinuity into American foreign policy. It created a sense of emergency that the

Bush administration skillfully exploited for its own purposes. Violations of American standards of behavior that would have been considered objectionable in normal times came to be accepted as appropriate to the circumstances, and the president has become immune to criticism, because it would be unpatriotic to criticize him when the nation is at war with terrorism. Contrary to the mission statement of the Project for the New American Century, our policies did not strengthen our ties to our democratic allies; on the contrary, they stand in the way of international cooperation. There has been an unprecedented rift between the United States and what Donald Rumsfeld calls "old Europe," because the United States demands unquestioning subservience from its allies. Some, like French President Jacques Chirac, resisted even to the point of endangering French national interests; others, like British Prime Minister Tony Blair, aligned themselves with us in the hope of modifying our behavior, but they have found themselves in an untenable position with regard to their electorates. It is difficult for a democracy like Britain to be allied with a country determined to act unilaterally.

The discontinuity was brought about by the Bush administration's carrying to extremes certain ideological tendencies that were already present in the United States before President Bush came into office. Ever since Senator Barry Goldwater's candidacy, the Republican Party has come under the domination of a curious alliance between religious fundamentalists and market fundamentalists. The two groups feed off each other—religious fundamentalism provides both an antidote to and a cover for the amorality of the market. Market fundamentalists and religious fundamentalists make strange bedfellows, but they have been held together by their success: Together they came to dominate the Republican Party.

Until recently, the natural complement of market fundamentalism in the foreign policy area has been geopolitical realism, which maintains that states should—and do—pursue their national interests. The pursuit of American supremacy is a wild extrapolation of that idea, reflecting America's success as the sole remaining superpower. The neoconservatives add a dose of proselytizing zeal that is lacking in geopolitical realists. Necons regard the American model of national success as superior to all others and want the rest of the world to benefit from it. That is the origin of the quaint idea that we can introduce democracy to a country like Iraq by military force. Although they were influential, the advocates of American supremacy could not have their way until the terrorists struck on September 11. That is when American foreign policy entered what I call *far-from-equilibrium* territory.

The country is now in the grip of an extremist ideology that is changing not only America's role in the world but the very character of the country. I call it extremist because I do not believe that it corresponds to the beliefs and values of the majority of Americans. Both the executive and the legislative branches of government are dominated by the same attitude, and President Bush is mounting a campaign to impose it on the judiciary. Disagreement is not tolerated. Government is run in a more authoritarian and ruthless manner than ever before. The moderate core of the Republican Party is being progressively eviscerated.* Criticism, which is essential to an open society, is stifled by being treated as unpatriotic. The policies of the Bush administration do not only affect America's posture in the world; domestically, they favor the rich to the detriment of the middle class and the poor and they reinforce the unholy alliance between the state and big business that was first identified by President Eisenhower as the military-industrial complex.

People are not aware of how dramatic the changes are, partly because the changes are seen as the continuation of tendencies that have been in effect for some time and partly because they are seen as a concomitant of the war on terrorism. Yet September 11 marks a transition when the abnormal, the radical, and the extreme became redefined as normal.

---

*When two moderate Republicans, Senators Olympia Snowe and George Voinovich, who are fiscal conservatives, insisted on limiting the size of the budget deficit, they were viciously attacked in TV ads. Snow was shown, ultimate disgrace, with a French flag.

CHAPTER **2**

The War on Terror

Terrorists pose an enormous threat to our national and personal security, and we must protect ourselves and our country from them. The suicide bombers of September 11 found us unprepared, and many of the measures we have taken since then are necessary and appropriate. Indeed, it can be argued that not enough has been done to prevent future attacks. But there is something fundamentally wrong with the Bush administration's war on terror. The war being waged has little to do with ending terrorism or enhancing homeland security; on the contrary, it uses terror as a pretext for waging war.

It is said that in the seventy-two hours following the terrorist attack, the Bush administration became engaged in an intense debate on how to respond to it. Eventually, the war terminology prevailed.*

War is a false and misleading metaphor in the context of combating terrorism. Treating the attacks of September 11 as crimes against humanity would have been more appropriate. Crimes require police work, not military action. To protect against terrorism, you need precautionary measures, awareness, and intelligence gathering—all of which ultimately depend on the support of the populations among which the terrorists operate. Imagine for a moment that September 11 had been treated as a crime. We would have pursued Bin Laden in Afghanistan, but we would not have invaded Iraq. Nor would we have our military struggling to perform police work in full combat gear and getting killed in the process.

Declaring war on terrorism suited the purposes of the Bush administration better because it invoked our military might. But it is the wrong way to deal with terrorism.[†] Military action requires an identifiable target, preferably a state. As a result, the war on terrorism has been directed

---

*Bob Woodward, *Bush at War* (New York: Simon and Schuster, 2002), 42.

[†]"[T]o use, or rather to misuse, the term 'war' is not simply a matter of legality or pedantic semantics. It has deeper and more dangerous consequences. To declare that one is at war is immediately to create a war psychosis that may be totally counterproductive for the objective being sought. It arouses an immediate expectation, and demand, for spectacular military action against some easily identifiable adversary, preferably a hostile state—action leading to decisive results" (Michael Howard, "What's in a Name? How to Fight Terrorism," *Foreign Affairs* 81, no. 1 [January/February 2002], p. 9).

primarily against states harboring terrorists. Yet terrorists are nonstate actors by definition, even if in many cases they are sponsored by a state. By turning the hunt for terrorists into a war, we are bound to create some innocent victims. The more innocent victims there are, the greater the resentment and the better the chances that some victims will turn perpetrators.

VICTIMS TURNING PERPETRATORS

Victims turning perpetrators is a well-known syndrome both in individuals and in groups.* Repressive rulers often exhibit a similar pattern. Both Mahathir bin Muhammad of Malaysia and Robert Mugabe of Zimbabwe appeal to the memory of colonial repression while engaging in repressive acts of varying severity.

Perhaps the most poignant and difficult case is Israel. Jews were the victims of the holocaust, which can itself be ascribed, in part, to a process of victims turning perpetrators: Hitler rose to power by capitalizing on a wave of resentment caused by an onerous peace treaty and runaway

*The idea was first popularized by Erich Fromm, *The Anatomy of Human Destructiveness* (New York: Holt, Rinehart and Winston, 1973). Criminologist Lonnie H. Athens, in *The Creation of Dangerous Violent Criminals* (New York: Routledge, 1989), later collected case studies of some of the most violent criminals in U.S. jails and found a recurrent pattern: An abused youth chooses a perpetrator as his role model and starts imitating him; when he finds that he can get away with it, he carries the violence to extremes.

inflation. He appealed to the German people's sense of being victimized. Whether the Germans' sense of victimization was imaginary or not, there can be no doubt that the Jews were victims in the literal sense. In the holocaust, many Jews went to their death helplessly and naively obeying orders, something I witnessed personally as a thirteen-year-old in Budapest.*

After the war, Jews resorted to terrorism against the British in Palestine in order to secure a homeland in Israel. Subsequently, after being attacked by Arab nations, Israel occupied additional territory and expelled many of the inhabitants. Eventually, the Arab victims also turned perpetrators, and Israel started suffering terrorist attacks. Israel made a habit of retaliating vigorously, enlarging the circle of Arab victims. Yitzhak Rabin made a valiant attempt to reverse the vicious cycle with the Oslo Accords of 1993, and he came very close to succeeding, so close that a Jewish extremist found it necessary to murder him in 1995. Subsequent attempts at reaching a settlement were rebuffed by Yasir Arafat, who thrived on conflict and recognized that a democratic Palestinian state at peace with Israel would likely mean the end of his days as leader.

---

*During that time, I was working for the Jewish Council in Budapest as a runner and I was instructed to deliver notices to Jewish lawyers to report at the Rabbinical Seminary with food and clothing the next day. When I showed the notices to my father, who was also a lawyer, he told me to warn the recipients that they were going to be deported. I informed one of the recipients, who replied, "They can't do that to me. I've always been a law-abiding citizen."

The situation deteriorated until suicide bombings became commonplace. Perpetrators are now in charge on both sides. The current Israeli prime minister, Ariel Sharon, has been held responsible for the massacre of Palestinians that took place in the Shatila and Sabra refugee camps in Lebanon in 1982. The Palestinians and Israel are locked in a vicious circle of escalating violence.

The policy of retaliation is not without its own logic. Terrorists need an organization and a source of outside support. If you can strike at the source, sometimes you can destroy the organization. Israel, with its excellent intelligence and total dedication to self-defense, was very successful in fending off terrorism for many years and executed many brilliant counterstrikes. Yet terrorism has not been eradicated. It reappeared whenever more peaceful methods of protest failed to produce positive results. In the Second Intifada, in Jenin, it took nearly six months, during which time some fifty inhabitants were killed, before the first suicide bomber emerged from that town. Subsequently, Jenin became a major source of suicide bombers. Jenin was then subjected to a siege in which twenty-three Israeli soldiers and an unknown number of inhabitants were killed.*

*A planned UN investigation was aborted when the Israeli government stated its opposition to the composition and mission of the fact-finding team appointed by the UN secretary-general. The team was prevented from carrying out any on-the-ground investigation (meeting only in Geneva) and was disbanded on May 3, 2002, when it became clear that Israel's objections could not be dealt with. A report on events in Jenin and other Palestinian areas was nevertheless prepared.

George Soros

Under the Bush administration, the United States has also become a victim-turned-perpetrator, although the American public would be loath to recognize it. On September 11, America was the victim of a heinous crime and the whole world expressed spontaneous and genuine sympathy. Since then, the war on terrorism has claimed more innocent civilians in Afghanistan and Iraq than have the attacks on the World Trade Center.* That comparison is rarely made at home: American lives are valued differently than the lives of foreigners, but the distinction is less obvious to people abroad.

ANTI-AMERICAN SENTIMENT

Indeed, since the United States has pursued the war on terror, world public opinion has turned sharply against us. The swing has been impressive. On September 12, 2001, a special meeting of the North Atlantic Council invoked Article 5 of the NATO Treaty for the first time in the alliance's history, calling on all member states to treat the

United Nations General Assembly, "Report of the Secretary-General prepared pursuant to General Assembly resolution ES-10/10," July 30, 2002. Available at: http://ods-dds-ny.un.org/doc/UNDOC/GEN/N02/499/57/IMG/N0249957.pdf? OpenElement

*For Iraq, the civilian casualties tabulated by Iraqi Body Count place total civilian deaths at between 7,377 and 9,180 (http://www.iraqbodycount.net). Similar tabulations of civilian deaths in Afghanistan stand at about 3,500 (http://pub-pages.unh.edu/%7Emwherold/).

terrorist attack on the United States as an attack upon their own soil. On September 13, 2001, *Le Monde*'s lead headline declared, *"Nous sommes tous américains"* ("We are all Americans") in a robust display of solidarity. The United Nations promptly endorsed punitive U.S. action against al Qaeda in Afghanistan.

A little more than a year later, the United States could not secure a UN resolution to authorize the invasion of Iraq, and in 2003, when we would have welcomed international involvement, we faced strong resistance. Surveys conducted in November 2002 revealed that fully one-third of all Britons viewed George Bush as a greater threat to world peace than Saddam Hussein, and attitudes have not improved since then.* A Pew Research Center poll released in March 2003 found that the percentage of the British population holding "favorable views" of the United States had declined drastically (from 75 percent to 48 percent) relative to levels measured in mid-2003.†

A large majority throughout the world opposed the war in Iraq. One and a half million Europeans took to the streets in mid-February 2003 to express opposition to the Iraqi war. In the meantime, Gerhard Schroeder secured reelection in Germany in September 2002 by refusing to

*Patrick Wintour and Ewen MacAskill, "One in Three Say Bush Is Biggest Threat," *Guardian*, November 14, 2002.
†The Pew Research Center for the People and the Press, "America's Image Further Erodes, Europeans Want Weaker Ties," March 18, 2003, 1, available at http://people-press.org/reports/pdf/175.pdf.

cooperate with the United States on Iraq. In a similar fashion, South Koreans elected an underdog candidate to the presidency because he was considered the least friendly to the United States. Surveys show that more South Koreans regard the United States as a greater danger to their security than North Korea. After the Coalition victory, most Iraqis were happy to be rid of Saddam, but that does not mean they welcome American occupation.

A reverse transformation has taken place in American public opinion. Immediately after September 11, America passed through a period of questioning and heart-searching. Newspaper op-eds and articles in both the popular press and academic journals sought to shed light on the sources of global anti-Americanism. Two years later, the mood has hardened and the U.S. public responds negatively to the hostility emanating from abroad. If the world increasingly regards the United States as a rogue superpower, many Americans seem to be holding fast to a self-image in which they are the victims. French President Jacques Chirac's threat to veto a UN Security Council resolution approving military action against Iraq gave rise to a spontaneous boycott of French goods among American consumers. The canteen of Congress has renamed French fries "freedom fries." Donald Rumsfeld's berating of "old Europe" has found a sympathetic audience. Even as the American public turns against President Bush, it continues to blame the French.

DELIBERATE DECEPTION

Usually when victims turn perpetrators, they are un-aware of what they are doing. That is the case with the American public today. Most people believe that terrorism poses a threat to our personal and national existence and that in waging war on terrorism we are acting in self-defense. The idea that we may have been transformed from victims to perpetrators must be rather shocking to most of us.

By contrast, the advocates of American supremacy within the Bush administration knew what they were doing when they advised President Bush to declare war on terrorism. This can be most clearly demonstrated in the case of the Iraqi invasion. As mentioned earlier, many of the key players in the Project for the New American Century argued for invading Iraq as early as 1998 in an open letter to President Clinton. After September 11, 2001, they claimed that Saddam Hussein was in possession of weapons of mass destruction and had links with al Qaeda. They were prepared to argue the case even if it involved deception and outright lies.

Clearly, there must have been other reasons for invading Iraq; otherwise, the neocon ideologues would not have advocated it as early as 1998. Those reasons remained unspoken. The invasion of Iraq had to be fitted into the context of the war on terrorism because that is what President Bush claimed a mandate to fight. The campaign of misinformation was led by President Bush

personally, although he may also have been deceived by
the people around him; one statement does not exclude
the other. The debate on Iraq was entirely stilted. The
possibility that the United States was motivated by considerations such as ensuring the flow of oil supplies could
not even be mentioned, because it would have been regarded as unpatriotic or worse.

The war on terrorism as pursued by the Bush administration cannot be won, because it is based on false pretenses.
The war on terrorism is more likely to bring about a permanent state of war. Terrorists are invisible; therefore, they will
never disappear. They will continue to provide a convenient pretext for the pursuit of American supremacy by military means. That pursuit, in turn, will continue to generate
resistance, setting up a vicious circle of escalating violence.

In this respect, there is a parallel between the war on terrorism and the war on drugs: The remedy is inappropriate
to the disease. In the case of drugs, we are confronted by a
public health problem, not a problem of crime. The public
health problem cannot be properly addressed if we treat
drug addicts as criminals. In the case of terrorists we *are*
dealing with a crime. We need detective work, good intelligence, and cooperation from the public, not military action. In both cases, waging war is a false metaphor that can
be used to justify repressive measures.*

*When I decided to extend the operations of my Open Society Foundation to
the United States, I chose drug policy as one of the first fields of engagement. I

REEXAMINING THE TERRORIST THREAT

Terrorism is not new. It was an important factor in nineteenth-century Russia, and it had a great influence in shaping the character of the czarist regime, enhancing the importance of the secret police and justifying authoritarian rule. More recently, several European countries—Italy, Germany, Spain, Greece, and the United Kingdom—have had to contend with terrorist gangs. It took each of them a decade or more to root them out, but they did not live in thrall of terrorism during all that time.

Using hijacked planes for suicide attacks *is* something new, and so is the potential for the terrorists' use of weapons of mass destruction. There is clear evidence that al Qaeda was experimenting with chemical and biological weapons in Afghanistan, and we must take the threat seriously. Suicide bombers using hijacked airplanes took us unawares; we cannot let that happen with nuclear, biological, or chemical weapons. To come to terms with these threats will require serious attention, but we cannot let them dominate our existence.

---

felt that drug policy was the area in which the United States was in the greatest danger of violating the principles of open society. I did not claim that I had all the right answers, but I was sure of one thing: The war on drugs was doing more harm than the drugs themselves—and on that point the evidence is clear. Drugs kill a few people, incapacitate many more, and give parents sleepless nights. On the other hand, the war on drugs has put millions behind bars, disrupted entire communities, particularly in the inner cities, and destabilized entire countries.

George Soros

It is high time to reconsider the war on terrorism. By allowing terrorism to become our principal preoccupation, we are playing straight into the terrorists' hands: They—and not us—are setting our priorities. September 11 needs to be put into the proper perspective. The loss of three thousand innocent lives is an enormous human tragedy, but it does not endanger our existence as a nation. To elevate the threat posed by al Qaeda to the level represented by nuclear war is a wild exaggeration that can be sustained only by cultivating a link between terrorism and weapons of mass destruction.

The expression *weapons of mass destruction* is itself a misnomer: Nuclear, chemical, and biological weapons have little in common.* As of now, chemical and biological weapons do not approach nuclear weapons in destructive power, although they do hold the menace of the unknown. They are also more easily accessible. We know that al Qaeda was experimenting with chemical and biological weapons in Afghanistan and Saddam Hussein actually used poison gas against his own people in 1975.

But terrorist groups cannot marshal the same resources as state-sponsored weapons programs can, and there is no evidence of any link between al Qaeda and Saddam Hus-

*At the inquiry into the suicide of the British weapons expert David Kelly, a Ministry of Defense official, Brian Jones, said, "I think 'weapons of mass destruction' has become a convenient catch-all which in my opinion can at times confuse discussion of the subject" (Brian Jones, quoted in Warren Hoge, "Arms Dossier Troubled British Experts, Panel Is Told," *New York Times*, September 4, 2003).

sein. It is highly unlikely that Saddam's Iraq would have dared to supply terrorists with weapons of mass destruction because of the repercussions: It is easier to find Iraq than the terrorists. The occurrence of an anthrax attack immediately following September 11, with anthrax of a high quality that only the U.S. weapons program was capable of producing, remains a strange and still unexplained incident, but undoubtedly it contributed to the myth that links weapons of mass destruction with terrorism. The anthrax attack had few victims; a portable nuclear bomb would have many more.

Exaggerating these threats only makes them worse. Yet that is exactly what the Bush administration is doing. When John Ashcroft accused a scruffy dropout named José Padillo of a plot to release a radioactive "dirty bomb," the attorney general achieved the same result as a terrorist perpetuating such a scheme: He fostered fear. Fear can be a useful tool in the hands of a government intent on exploiting it: It unites people against a common enemy. Communism used to serve as the enemy; now terrorism can fill the role. The appeal to patriotism can also be used to silence the critics. We seem to have come a long way from the time when President Roosevelt reminded the nation that "the only thing we have to fear is fear itself."

The important thing to remember about terrorism is that it is a reflexive phenomenon: Its impact and development are precisely dependent on the actions and reactions of the victims. If the victims react by turning into perpetrators, terrorism triumphs in the sense of engendering a vicious cycle of escalating violence. That is what the fanatically militant Islamists who perpetrated September 11 must have hoped to achieve.

A Different Vision for America

The most powerful country on earth cannot afford to be consumed by fear. To make the war on terrorism the centerpiece of our national strategy is an abdication of our responsibility as the leading nation in the world. The United States is the only country that can take the lead in addressing problems that require collective action: preserving peace, assuring economic progress, protecting the environment, and so on. Fighting terrorism and controlling weapons of mass destruction also fall into this category.

The United States cannot do whatever it wants, but nothing much can be done in the way of international cooperation without the leadership or at least active participation of our nation. The United States has a greater degree of discretion in deciding what shape the world should take than anybody else. Other countries have to respond to U.S. policy, but we can choose the policy to which others have to respond. This imposes a unique responsibility on the United States: Our nation must concern itself with the well-being of the world. We will be the greatest beneficiaries if we do so.

CHAPTER 3

The Bush Administration's Foreign Policy

Not only does the Bush administration pursue the wrong goals but, even in terms of its own objectives, its policies have been remarkably counterproductive. This is particularly evident in foreign policy, but it also applies to domestic affairs.

During his 2000 campaign for the presidency, George W. Bush claimed that he stood for a "humble" foreign policy and opposed foreign intervention aimed at nation building. These were the slogans that stuck in the public mind at the time. Behind this bland surface lurked a well-thought-out and rather aggressive concept of America's role in the world. The Republican Party foreign policy platform on which Bush was running harked back to the halcyon days of the Cold War, when the United States was both super-power and leader of the free world.* The platform was built on the idea that the Clinton administration had failed to use America's position as the sole remaining superpower to full advantage and that the best way for the United States to regain unilateral control over its destiny lay through the development and deployment of a missile defense system. Although the platform did not make this point explicit, the militarization of space would give the United States control over the globe. We could project our power to distant parts, such as the Taiwan Straits, without fear of reprisal from the growing number of states equipped with long-range missiles. We could then decide whom to defend when.

In Search of an Enemy

With the demise of the Soviet Union, the only thing missing was a suitable enemy. North Korea was deemed sufficient to justify the first phase of the missile defense program; therefore, it had to be kept out in the cold. South Korean President Kim Dae Jung was one of the first heads of state to visit President Bush in the White House in March 2001. South Korea had engaged North Korea in a "sunshine policy" of rapprochement and improved diplomatic

*Republican National Committee, "Principled American Leadership," available at http://www.rnc.org/GOPInfo/Platform/2000platform8.htm.

ties, and President Kim was eager to obtain President Bush's endorsement. President Kim had the support of the State Department, but was rebuffed by President Bush, who publicly announced his intention to suspend efforts aimed at concluding a missile agreement and normalizing U.S.–North Korean relations.* And so began the current North Korean nuclear crisis.

While North Korea could serve as the enemy for the first phase of the national missile defense program, China was being groomed as the enemy for the later phases. Conservative Republicans had for some time stressed the dangers of China's rising economic and military capability. Whereas Clinton and his foreign policy team labeled China a "strategic partner," the Bush administration tended to view China as something closer to a strategic rival. In addition to China, Russia was another possible adversary held in reserve by missile defense advocates.

At the same time, the Bush administration made its

---

*President Bush justified this break with Clinton administration policy: "We're not certain as to whether or not they're keeping all terms of all agreements." This caused confusion on all sides. Not only did North Korea and the United States have only one agreement—the 1994 accord that ended North Korea's nuclear program in exchange for U.S. assistance in the construction of light reactors suitable for civilian uses—but senior officials confirmed shortly after the president's statement that North Korea appeared to be honoring its commitments. See David E. Sanger, "Bush Tells Seoul Talks with North Korea Won't Resume Now," *New York Times*, March 8, 2001. Later on, North Korea announced that it had a secret uranium enrichment program. To add to the complexity of the situation, that program did not actually violate the letter of the 1994 accord, which related only to plutonium.

aversion to international treaties abundantly clear by re-
nouncing the Kyoto Protocol on global warming and
rejecting the verification protocol to the Biological Weapons Convention, in each case offering no alternatives. Not
only did the Bush administration reject the International
Criminal Court (ICC), but it embarked on an active campaign to sabotage it. The administration applied tremendous pressure on its allies to sign bilateral agreements one
by one, exempting American citizens. Countries like Alba-
nia and Romania succumbed in spite of countervailing
pressure from the European Union.* Altogether, during
the first year of the Bush presidency, there was a conscious
effort to create a discontinuity with the Clinton policies
wherever possible. The Bush administration threatened to
withdraw from the Balkans and took a hands-off approach
to the peace process in the Middle East.

Once September 11 provided President Bush with the
enemy he was looking for, he became a man with an or-
dained mission. It suited his personality. Being a reformed
substance abuser and born-again Christian, he had personal
acquaintance with the devil. The devil took the form of suicide bombers who tried to destroy him personally in the
White House; this gave him an intensely felt sense of personal engagement. He no longer read prepared speeches in a
hesitant manner; he no longer stumbled over words, and

*Aryeh Neier, President of the Open Society Institute, estimates that up to $100
million in military aid was tied to these bilateral agreements.

the public appreciated his certitude. Prior to the terrorist attack, he had been a figurehead; a few days after September 11, he rose to be a leader—one who believed that he had been given a historic task. The trouble is that he is leading us—and the world—in the wrong direction.

HIJACKING SEPTEMBER 11

September 11 would have offered an excellent opportunity to gather public support for improving the world order. It brought home the realization that all is not well beyond our borders. We are spending $160 billion in Iraq; a small fraction of that sum could have made a tremendous difference if used in a constructive way around the world. But nothing could have been further from the Bush administration's mind. The proponents of a "New American Century" saw the world as a struggle for survival and believed that the United States, having proved itself the fittest, had both the right and duty to impose its will on the world. They abhorred soft-heartedness, tolerance, and affirmative action. As reflected in the very name of their project, they had advocated the pursuit of American military dominance even before President Bush came into office. September 11 gave them the opportunity to implement their ideas.

At home, Attorney General John Ashcroft rammed the

George Soros

Patriot Act through Congress by declaring that those who opposed it were giving aid and comfort to the enemy. Nancy Chang describes the process:

> In a last-minute exercise of brute force, the Republican House leadership jettisoned an antiterrorism bill that raised far fewer civil liberties concerns and that had been unanimously approved by the House Judiciary Committee, and replaced it with the 342-page USA PATRIOT Act.* Congress passed this legislation with breathtaking speed at a moment when it was exiled from its anthrax-contaminated offices and the nation was on edge from Attorney General John Ashcroft's predictions of more terrorist attacks. President George W. Bush signed it into law on October 26, 2001, only six weeks after the September 11 attacks. Legislators complained that they did not have time to obtain, much less read, a copy of the act before it was brought to a vote. To make matters worse, this complex and far-reaching legislation was accompanied by little public hearing or debate and by no conference or committee report. In the House, the act passed by the wide margin of 356 to 66. In the Senate, Senator Russell Feingold cast the lone opposition vote. As he did so, he warned

*The USA PATRIOT Act is an acronym for Uniting and Strengthening America by Providing Appropriate Tools Required to Intercept and Obstruct Terrorism Act of 2001.

the nation, "Preserving our freedom is one of the main reasons that we are now engaged in this new war on terrorism. We will lose that war without firing a shot if we sacrifice the liberties of the American people."*

The Patriot Act confers unprecedented powers on the executive branch and removes many of the constraints imposed by judicial processes. Taken together with its companion piece, the Homeland Security Act, it limits public access to government information while at the same time promoting government access to sensitive personal information and sharing that information among federal, state, and local authorities. Although the legislation seriously infringes civil liberties, it aroused little concern in the public because most of the legislation's provisions are assumed to be directed against *them*, terrorists and foreigners, rather than *us*, innocent civilians. Perhaps the only infringement that visibly touches everyone is the invasion of privacy—the expanded ability of the federal government to wiretap, monitor e-mail, and track library checkout records—but this incursion may be considered a small price to pay for protection against terrorism. Nevertheless, the Patriot Act opens the way to serious abuses of power. A number of accused terrorists have been induced

*Nancy Chang, "How Democracy Dies: The War on Our Civil Liberties," in *Lost Liberties: Ashcroft and the Assault on Personal Freedom*, ed. Cynthia Brown (New York and London: New Press, 2003), p. 33-51.

to plead guilty by the threat of being removed from the judicial process altogether, detained for long periods without trial or subjected to secret military tribunals. The United States has detained and deported visitors and immigrants without recourse; prisoners caught in Afghanistan are kept in cages at Guantanamo Bay and denied the protection of the Geneva Conventions.

And the threat, as the *New York Times* has reported, is increasing:

> The government is using its expanded authority under the far-reaching law to investigate suspected drug traffickers, white-collar criminals, blackmailers, child pornographers, money launderers, spies and even corrupt foreign leaders, federal officials said.
>
> Justice Department officials says they are simply using all the tools now available to them to pursue criminals—terrorists or otherwise. But critics of the administration's antiterrorism tactics assert that such use of the law is evidence the administration is using terrorism as a guise to pursue a broader law enforcement agenda.*

This is all the more troubling because Ashcroft has demonstrated his intolerance in other fields. He has banned plea bargaining and introduced a system of keep-

---

*Eric Lichtblau, "U.S. Uses Terror Law to Pursue Crimes from Drugs to Swindling," *New York Times*, September 28, 2003.

ing tabs on lenient judges. He has aggressively infringed the rights of states to legislate and enforce provisions on issues such as gun control and medical marijuana.*

One of the most insidious ways in which the Bush administration is seeking to undermine established liberties is through the nomination of right-wing ideologues as federal judges. Normally when a nomination is blocked in Congress because of the political views of the nominee, the president comes back with a more moderate candidate. Under the Bush administration, one nominee is more extreme than the other. The Democrats have conducted an effective filibuster in the Senate on two candidates and threaten to do so on others, but the majority of the president's far-right nominees do slip through. The public does not seem to pay much attention, because no Supreme Court seat is at stake.

THE AXIS OF EVIL

In foreign affairs, the war on terrorism has taken precedence over all other considerations—although, significantly, there has been no slowdown in the national missile

---

*Ibid.; and Eric Lichtblau, "Justice Department to Monitor Judges for Sentences Shorter Than Guidelines Suggest," *New York Times*, August 7, 2003. See also American Civil Liberties Union, "Insatiable Appetite: The Government's Demand for New and Unnecessary Powers After September 11th," available at http://www.aclu.org/SafeandFree/SafeandFree.cfm?ID=10623&c=207.

defense program. Because war has to be waged against someone and terrorists are difficult to find, it is easier to identify states that might harbor terrorists. It is this logic that led to the invention of an "axis of evil" in the 2002 state-of-the-union speech.

Of the three countries included in the president's axis, only one—Iran—has well-established links with international terrorism. There can be no doubt that the three countries singled out in the speech are evil, but lumping them together and leaving out some other prize specimens like Syria, Libya, Zimbabwe, Burma (Myanmar), Uzbekistan, and Turkmenistan gives rise to the same kind of distortion as does declaring war on terrorism. North Korea is the most tightly closed society in the world; people there are ruthlessly oppressed and all resources are devoted to building up military power. While it has no connection with the terrorist attack on September 11, North Korea has a dangerous missile and nuclear capability and a track record of selling arms abroad.* Saddam Hussein's Iraq was equally repressive, but he did not pose the

*In his Axis of Evil speech, President Bush nevertheless sought to rhetorically link North Korea with the events of September 11 through the conflation of terrorism with the possession of weapons of mass destruction and with other misdeeds as well: "Our . . . goal is to prevent regimes that sponsor terror from threatening America or our friends and allies with weapons of mass destruction. Some of these regimes have been pretty quiet since September the 11th. But we know their true nature. North Korea is a regime arming with missiles and weapons of mass destruction while starving its citizens" (George W. Bush, "President's State of the Union Address," U.S. Capitol, Washington, D.C., January 29, 2002, available at http://www.whitehouse.gov/news/releases/2002/01/20020129-11.html).

same military threat. While he unquestionably used chemical weapons to kill his own people, he had subsequently been defeated in a war during which no chemical or biological weapons were used. Nor does Iraq have a nuclear capability. Saddam has given rewards to families of Palestinian suicide bombers, but—contrary to the administration's assertions—he had no proven ties to al Qaeda.

Iran is a more complicated case than the other two. It is ruled by a Shiite theocracy that is fundamentally opposed to both America and Israel, but the people have had enough of Islamic fundamentalism. They have elected a reformist president and parliament, and the adherents of open society are more fervent and willing to make greater sacrifices in Iran than in the United States. But the reformers have been unable to deliver, because the judiciary and the so-called power ministries—army, police, and intelligence—are in the hands of hard-liners. Publications are regularly closed down, critics of the regime put in jail and occasionally murdered. President Khatami's failure to oppose the hard-liners more forcefully has begun to erode the public's confidence in his ability to achieve meaningful reforms.

In the meantime Iran continues to support Hezbollah, the terrorist movement based in Lebanon; has attempted to supply arms to Arafat in Palestine; and is engaged in a far-reaching nuclear development program. Iran remains a party to the Nuclear Non-Proliferation Treaty (NPT) and claims that its nuclear program is intended for strictly civilian purposes, but inspections carried out under the NPT have found its program to be in violation of treaty provisions. In terms of nuclear weapons, Iran is much more dangerous than Iraq has been for more than a decade.

Each of the three countries presents a different set of problems. Lumping them together as the Axis of Evil is misleading and counterproductive. They will not all respond to the same strategy. In the case of Iran, the Axis of Evil speech has served only to strengthen that country's domestic forces who oppose the development of an open and democratic society.

AFGHANISTAN

The invasion of Afghanistan was justified by its role as the home base of al Qaeda. The Afghan operation had the support of the international community and took place with UN approval. Even before the invasion, a political process was put in place to establish a provisional government. It started with a conference near Bonn, Germany, in November 2001 and culminated in the Loya Jirga inside Afghanistan on June 11, 2002. The Hamid Karzai government enjoys some measure of legitimacy.*

*I provided seed money to a working group that helped prepare the political process. It was headed by Barnett Rubin of New York University's Center on International Cooperation and Ashraf Ghani, a former World Bank official, who subsequently became finance minister in the Karzai government.

The invasion of Afghanistan was a brilliant demonstration of the newfound military prowess of the United States. The smart bombs had gotten a lot smarter since the 1991 Gulf War, and the use of Special Forces constituted an important tactical advance. The United States demonstrated that its military capabilities were greater than ever. At the same time, the operation failed to produce the positive results that could have been attained.

First, the Special Forces failed to find bin Laden. This shows one of the limitations from which America suffers in waging war. We may have all the military power in the world, but we do not want to take casualties. As a result, much of the hunt was subcontracted out to local warlords, who proved unreliable.* The initial assault on Tora Bora, a large cave complex on the Afghan-Pakistan border, where bin Laden was supposed to have taken refuge, involved only Afghan forces supported by American air power. American ground forces did not arrive in the region until three days into the battle, by which time it was discovered that large numbers of the Taliban and al Qaeda had slipped or bribed their way through the surrounding cordon of Afghan forces. When remaining elements of the Taliban and al Qaeda were later isolated in the Shah-I-Kot valley, Operation Anaconda saw a much greater reliance on American troops. Nevertheless, most of the terrorists escaped.

*Another possible explanation is that U.S. troops were being reserved for the invasion of Iraq.

Second, the Bush administration has failed to win the peace. It could have drawn upon the experiences gained in the Balkans and done better than either in Bosnia or in Kosovo, but the administration was hampered by its visceral aversion to international cooperation and by the opposition to nation building that George W. Bush enunciated in his presidential campaign.

The opportunity was present. The people of Afghanistan were desperate for assistance, and the various agencies of the United Nations were well established on the ground with many local employees. The international community was willing to commit large amounts of money at a donors' conference. The task of overseeing and administering these funds ought to have been entrusted to the United Nations. UN agents could have fanned out into the villages, accompanied by peacekeepers safeguarding the money the agents would carry with them. They would have been welcomed with open arms. They could have set up local administrations on behalf of the Karzai government, and the warlords would have lost their influence because they could not have competed in providing services.*

The Bush administration had different ideas. The Defense Department was not concerned with nation building but with hunting down bin Laden, and it needed the help of local warlords to do so. It did not want UN peacekeep-

---

*I argued for this approach in "Assembling Afghanistan," *Washington Post*, December 3, 2001.

ers traipsing around outside Kabul and getting in the way of U.S. forces and their ostensible Afghan allies. I questioned Donald Rumsfeld publicly on the subject at a conference in April 2002. At first he denied that he was opposed to UN peacekeepers outside Kabul, but later he admitted that he did not like the idea of a multiyear, multinational peacekeeping operation similar to Kosovo. He advocated setting up a national army and police force.

The results are there for all to see. Instead of a brilliant demonstration of what international assistance can do for a Muslim country, there has been very little progress in the region and the initial enthusiasm with which the overthrow of the Taliban was greeted has dissipated. The United States is belatedly allocating a billion dollars to reconstruction in Afghanistan, but most of the pledges made at the donors' conference have not been honored. The delivery of aid is hampered by the lack of security, and power remains largely in the hands of local warlords. Two years after American intervention, Afghanistan remains unstable and the Taliban are reasserting themselves in the Pushtun areas in the south. It has been argued that the invasion of Iraq diverted attention from Afghanistan, and that is undoubtedly true, but the reconstruction of Afghanistan would have been a flop in any case because of Rumsfeld's decision not to allow UN peacekeepers outside Kabul.

Now that NATO has taken charge, it may send troops

outside Kabul, but the historic moment when a different Afghanistan could have been born has passed. Afghanistan produced a bumper crop of opium in 2002, estimated at 3,400 tons.* Drugs account for at least half the economy. Income from drugs is estimated at $2.5 billion; this compares with foreign aid in the neighborhood of $2 billion.† It is difficult to see how the central government can assert control over warlords engaged in the drug trade. The depredations of the warlords combined with covert support from the tribal areas of Pakistan in promoting the revival of the Taliban.

Promoting Democracy

The invasion of Afghanistan required the establishment of military bases in neighboring countries. This has had an ambivalent effect on political conditions in those countries.** Each country is different, with oil and other natural resources or their absence exercising a decisive influence on local conditions; all of them, however, have a common tendency toward the erosion of freedoms gained from the collapse of the Soviet Union. The region is characterized

*Ahmed Rashid, *Far Eastern Economic Review*, October 16, 2003.
†Estimates provided verbally by the International Crisis Group (www.crisisweb.org).
**My foundation network has a strong presence in Central Asia and the Caucasus, and I visited the area in May–June 2003 to see the regional situation firsthand.

by lifetime presidencies and incipient dynastic successions. Increased American military presence has brought with it some much-needed increase in financial and technical assistance, but these resources are earmarked for military cooperation rather than political reform.

The U.S. government has displayed some sensitivity about becoming too closely identified with repressive regimes and has in some cases exercised a moderating influence on local governments. In Georgia, the Bush administration has asserted welcome pressure to insure that the forthcoming elections should be free and fair*. On balance, however, American involvement in the region has served primarily to reinforce repressive regimes, although within limits, because the United States could be embarrassed if a regime with which it is associated oversteps the mark.

Uzbekistan is especially troubling. President Islam Karimov has been ruthless in repressing all Islamic political manifestations. Large numbers were put in jail for not much more than having a beard. The Islamic Movement of Uzbekistan, a terrorist group closely allied with al Qaeda and the Taliban, actively opposed the regime in the late 1990s, but most of its membership was wiped out in Af-

---

*It failed to do so in Azerbaijan. Richard Armitage, deputy secretary of state, phoned Ilham Aliyev to congratulate him on his election as president of Azerbaijan before independent U.S. observers reported widespread fraud and intimidation in the elections. Guy Dinmore, "US calls for inquiry into Azerbaijan election," *Financial Times* (U.S. ed.), October 22, 2003.

ghanistan. This provided an opening for the regime to ease up and allow the Party of Liberation (Hizb-ut-Tahrir), a nonviolent Islamic movement, to function legally. But President Karimov failed to rise to the occasion and has continued his repression of religious groups and individuals. This behavior did not stop the United States from building up its military alliance with the regime.

President Pervez Musharraf of Pakistan became a close ally of the United States, although his pretense at holding democratic elections was hollow and his ability to perform in the war against terrorism is open to question. Having been deceived by our alliance with Saudi Arabia, we are exposing ourselves to a similar risk in Pakistan because Musharraf has to carefully navigate between our demands and domestic pressures from Islamic militants.

The war on terrorism has also had some accidental benefits. Relations with China have thawed out, giving the reformers there greater leverage over the hard-liners. Relations with Russia have improved too: President Bush met with President Vladimir Putin, looked into his soul, and liked what he saw. Whether this is all to the good is questionable, however, because Putin's soul is less democratic than Boris Yeltsin's was. Putin's treatment of the press, his policy in Chechnya, and his reassertion of state power over the oligarchs and regional governments raise serious questions about his commitment to freedom or democracy, let alone the principles of an open society.

The war on terrorism has, on balance, taken precedence over the promotion of political and economic reforms and failed to advance the cause of democracy. This is all the more reprehensible because promoting democracy has emerged as the main justification for invading Iraq.

The second Iraqi war had a particularly negative effect on the nascent democracy of Turkey. The government of the country is in the hands of a moderate Islamic Justice and Development Party (AK Party). The AK is genuinely devoted to making Turkey a more open society that would qualify for membership in the European Union. That is a rare phenomenon worthy of support. The army is very powerful and suspicious of the AK. The United States, eager for Turkish cooperation in the invasion of Iraq, struck a deal to which the government agreed but for which it could not gain majority support in Parliament. The deal was democratically rejected. This was a major setback for our military plans. Subsequently, Paul Wolfowitz went to Turkey and publicly reprimanded the generals for failing to exercise more influence—not a democracy-boosting exercise in a country with a long history of military coups.*

In fostering international cooperation, our war on terror

---

*Paul Wolfowitz, "Deputy Secretary of Defense Wolfowitz interview with CNN Turk," May 6, 2003, transcript available at http://www.dod.mil/transcripts/2003/tr20030506-depsecdef0156.html.

has been decidedly counterproductive. It may have helped U.S. relations with China and Russia, both of which like the idea of waging war on terror, but the war caused an unprecedented rift with our erstwhile allies. Public opinion in the rest of the world became deeply resentful of the Bush administration's unilateral ways. As we have seen, the attitude toward America has shifted 180 degrees from the immediate aftermath of September 11 to the invasion of Iraq.

CHAPTER 4

The Iraqi Quagmire

THE MOTIVES

The true motives for the Bush administration's determination to overthrow Saddam Hussein remain shrouded in mystery. It is possible to conjecture what these motives were, but it is impossible to identify them with certainty, because they have never been discussed. Nevertheless, it is worth looking back in order to better understand the roots of today's quagmire in Iraq.

One motive may have been the assertion of American supremacy—a demonstration that the United States sets the agenda. Iraq may have been chosen as a demonstration project for the simple reason that it was doable. Bob Woodward summarizes Deputy Secretary of Defense Paul Wolfowitz's comments at a key September 15, 2001, strategy session:

George Soros

Attacking Afghanistan would be uncertain. He worried about 100,000 American troops bogged down in mountain fighting in Afghanistan six months from then. In contrast, Iraq was a brittle, oppressive regime that might break easily, it was doable. He estimated that there was a 10 to 50 percent chance Saddam was involved in the September 11 terrorist attacks. The US would have to go after Saddam at some time if the war on terrorism was to be taken seriously.*

In an interview in May 2003, Wolfowitz said that while several factors lay behind the administration's policy, "for bureaucratic reasons we settled on one issue, weapons of mass destruction, because it was the one reason everyone could agree on."†

Taken on its own this would be hubris of the worst kind. But there are more realistic geopolitical considerations that can be adduced in favor of toppling Saddam. Perhaps the single most important impediment to America's control of its own destiny is its reliance on foreign oil. Saudi Arabia has proven itself a treacherous ally: It had maintained political stability at home by supporting Islamic extremism abroad. In the aftermath of September 11, this balancing act was no longer possible and the Saudi regime

*Bob Woodward, *Bush at War* (New York: Simon & Schuster, 2002), 83.
†Paul Wolfowitz, quoted in Sam Tanenhaus, "Bush's Brain Trust," *Vanity Fair*, July 2003, 169.

was in danger of becoming as unstable as the Shah's Iran had been. Iraq is strategically located, and its oil reserves are second only to those of Saudi Arabia. By occupying Iraq and moving American military bases from Saudi Arabia to Iraq, the United States could establish a secure alternative to Saudi oil. There was another factor to be taken into account. Global oil supplies were becoming increasingly tight, and the spigot on Iraqi oil had to be reopened sooner or later. But to lift the embargo with Saddam Hussein still in power might have made him too dangerous; therefore, he had to be removed from power.

The other important consideration was Israel. A large number of religious fanatics in the United States believe that the rebirth of Israel presages the apocalypse and the second coming of the Messiah. Hence, in addition to the traditional pro-Israel lobby, Israel also has strong support from the evangelical right—and that is the core of the president's constituency. Since the apocalypse involves the destruction of Israel, Israel might be better off without friends like this. President Bush, however, felt obliged to pay attention to his constituency. Establishing a strong military presence in Iraq would help to transform the political complexion of the entire region. This would reassure Israel and weaken the Palestinian extremists sufficiently to allow some progress toward a settlement on terms acceptable to Israel and its U.S. supporters. All of Europe, including Britain's Tony Blair, considered the issue of Palestine the top priority, but President Bush wanted to deal with Iraq first. This was a major source of conflict between the United States and Europe and led to an American commitment, which has not been kept, to give high priority to a Middle East peace settlement after the war.*

Oil and Israel likely loomed large in the administration's policy deliberations, but these were not the reasons publicly offered by Bush and his advisers for the invasion of Iraq. A person could not even raise these issues without being called unpatriotic. President Bush received a mandate for waging war against terrorism. Only by skillfully weaving the themes of terrorism and weapons of mass destruction together and raising the specter of terrorists gaining access to weapons of mass destruction could the president justify going to war with Iraq. Whatever the case for invading Iraq, the American public has every reason to feel deceived.

The Preparations

Internally, the Bush administration had been divided on the issue of invading Iraq. The hawks, concentrated in the Department of Defense, were unconditionally com-

*The conflict between Europe and the United States was sharpened by the fact that the far right in Europe is anti-Israel whereas the far right in America is pro-Israel—and the far right is in power in the United States.

mitted. They had their own timetable and did not want to get bogged down in a UN process that might have interfered with their timetable. In any case, as American supremacists, they were ideologically opposed to depending on the United Nations. By contrast, the State Department was anxious to ensure the legitimacy of military intervention. The hawks had the upper hand because they enjoyed the allegiance of the vice president and the ear of the president. A resolution authorizing the president to take whatever action he considered appropriate was rammed through Congress with the complicity of some Democrats, notably Congressman Richard Gephardt and Senator Joseph Lieberman, preempting a more measured and restrictive resolution in preparation by the leaders of the Senate Foreign Affairs Committee, Senators Joseph Biden and Richard Lugar.

At the United Nations, the other permanent members of the UN Security Council, particularly France, were eager for the Security Council to play an active role. As the drumbeat of war grew louder, the Security Council managed to agree on Resolution 1441 in November 2002. The resolution was carefully crafted so that the question of whether the United States had to return to the United Nations for authorization before engaging in military action was left open. The French managed to convince the Americans that the United States had something to gain and nothing to lose from agreeing to this formula. If Saddam Hussein violated the resolution, there would be no problem in passing a second resolution; indeed, the French would join the United States in military action. If Saddam complied with the resolution, yet the United States remained determined to go to war, it could still do so; the moment when the United States bypassed the United Nations would be merely postponed.

The resolution itself imposed a tough inspection regime and put the burden on Iraq to prove that it did not possess weapons of mass destruction. The good-cop/bad-cop routine between the two factions in the Bush administration had served a useful purpose: It showed how effective the Security Council could be with strong U.S. leadership. If the objective of American policy had truly been to control Iraq's weapons of mass destruction, that could have been achieved by continued inspections. But that is not what the Bush administration was interested in; it was determined to remove Saddam.

The UN inspectors found no evidence of any weapons of mass destruction, and as Hans Blix (executive chairman of the UN Monitoring, Verification and Inspection Commission) put it, Saddam was cooperative in the process but not on the substance. Saddam failed to provide an accounting of the destruction of the material that he was known to have possessed. Nevertheless, when Blix ruled that certain missiles exceeded the legal limit imposed on their range, the Iraqis started to comply with the order to destroy them. The United States, however, was set to go ahead with the invasion. When he was told about it, President Chirac of France took umbrage. He sent his foreign minister to the Security Council and threatened to veto a second resolution. Secretary of State Colin Powell took this as a betrayal of trust and joined forces with the hardliners within the administration. Using questionable evidence, he accused Iraq of violating UN Resolution 1441. France then actively lobbied against a new resolution, and the United States had to go ahead with the invasion without UN authorization.

The Invasion

The invasion itself was a resounding military success. It was accomplished faster and with fewer casualties than planned, even in the absence of Turkish participation. Moreover, after the military victory, the Security Council passed a second resolution (1483), which recognized the occupation of Iraq and provided a legal basis for it. Neither France, where President Chirac was under fire for hurting French commercial interests, nor Germany, which was eager to mend fences, dared to raise any objections. Indeed, Resolution 1483 went further than any previous UN resolution in retroactively legalizing unauthorized military action. In effect, the resolution conferred most of the attributes of Iraqi sovereignty upon the occupying powers for an indefinite period. It can be argued that this goes beyond the limits of existing international law, but the resolution cannot be deemed illegal because under international law, the UN Security Council has legislative powers. The ideologues of American supremacy have been arguing that international relations are relations of power and that international law merely legitimizes what power has wrought; with regard to Iraq, they were proven right.

In other respects, however, they were wrong. The arguments they used to justify the invasion—Saddam's possession of weapons of mass destruction and his connection to al Qaeda—turned out to be unsubstantiated or downright false. When the weapons of mass destruction could not be found, President Bush fell back on the justification of liberating Iraq from a heinous dictator and introducing democracy. That is indeed a noble cause, which could have justified the invasion if the president had made a case for it. But that was not the case that President Bush had presented to Congress, and presumably, Congress would not have endorsed it.

Democracy and open society are very difficult to establish, even if people have the best of intentions. With all the experience I have gained in various parts of the world, I would consider Iraq the last place to chose for a demonstration project. Iraq has no experience of democracy, and it is rife with latent ethnic and religious conflicts. Like many states of the Middle East, Iraq was artificially created by the Western powers after the disintegration of the Ottoman empire so as to allow the greatest possible scope for Western influence. Three *vilayets* of the Ottoman empire were combined to form Iraq. The Kurds, who constituted a majority in the north, were divided between Turkey, Iraq, and Iran. A Sunni majority around Baghdad was combined with a Shiite majority around Basra and the marshlands. A number of other ethnic and religious minorities were dispersed throughout Iraq. A Sunni-Hashemite king, brother of the king of Transjordania, was imposed on this concoction. When the monarchy was overthrown in 1958, the subsequent regimes maintained the political domination of the Sunni minority with ever-more repressive methods.

In light of the ethnic and religious divisions, the introduction of democracy could easily lead to the disintegration of the country. It was this consideration, reinforced by pressure from the neighboring Arab rulers, that stopped the first President Bush short of unseating Saddam in the first Gulf War. That was the hornet's nest that the second President Bush stirred up when he invaded Iraq. Introducing democracy was clearly not uppermost in his mind. As mentioned before, the real motives remain shrouded in mystery but nation building could not have ranked high among them. After all, circumstances were

George Soros

much more favorable in Afghanistan, but the Bush administration failed to take advantage of them. One of the reasons I was so opposed to the invasion of Iraq was that the action was liable to give nation building a bad name.

THE AFTERMATH

As I mentioned earlier, it is difficult to understand how President Bush could have embarked on the second Gulf War with so little forethought about, and preparation for, the aftermath. There had been plenty of warnings both from those responsible for the first Gulf War and from our European allies.* But the customary caution of geopolitical realists yielded to the arrogance of the American supremacists ensconced in the Defense Department. They cooked up their plans in secret and did not expose them to the sunlight of public discussion. As brilliant as the military part of the plan was, the aftermath has been a dismal failure. Apparently, the planners had expected the Iraqi army to stay out of the fray and hoped to preserve it so that it could provide the mainstay for security afterward. A rather shady Iraqi émigré, Ahmed Challabi, was groomed to become

"Trying to eliminate Saddam, extending the ground war into an occupation of Iraq . . . would have incurred incalculable human and political cost . . . We would have been forced to occupy Baghdad and, in effect, rule Iraq. The coalition would instantly have collapsed, the Arabs deserting it in anger and other allies pulling out as well." George Bush and Brent Scowcroft, *A World Transformed* (New York: Knopf, 1998), p. 489.

the head of an Iraqi interim authority, and the émigré son of a prominent Shiite cleric, Abdul Majid Al-Khoei, was supposed to assume leadership of the Shiite community.

That is not what happened. During the invasion, some Fedayeen Saddam put up resistance, but the rest of the armed forces, including the elite Republican Guards, melted away under the onslaught. Military occupation was followed by uncontrolled looting, and the victory turned into shambles. Upon returning, Al-Khoei was promptly murdered in the mosque in Najaf. The Iraqi population—far from greeting the Americans as liberators—became increasingly resentful.

Saddam Hussein appears to have planned on waging a guerrilla war. He may have had that in mind as early as October 2002, when he released all the prisoners from Iraqi jails. The guerrilla tactics forced the invaders to behave like occupying powers, suspicious of the civilian population and inflicting insults and injuries that turned the population against them. Iraq also acted as a magnet, attracting terrorists trained by al Qaeda in Afghanistan. With the Saudi authorities cracking down on them, sleeper cells in Saudi Arabia woke up and moved to Iraq, escalating the violence. Saddam Hussein had nothing to do with September 11, but President Bush has a point when he says that Iraq has become the central front in the war on terror—although killing soldiers qualifies as guerrilla warfare, not terrorism.

George Soros

It is hard to imagine how the plans of the Defense Department could have gone more awry. I had been prepared for unintended adverse consequences, but reality has far exceeded my imagination. We find ourselves in a quagmire that is in some ways reminiscent of Vietnam. Having invaded Iraq, we cannot extricate ourselves. Domestic pressure for withdrawing is likely to build, just as it did in the Vietnam War, but withdrawing would inflict irreparable damage on our standing in the world. In this respect, Iraq is worse than Vietnam because of our dependence on Middle Eastern oil.

It could have been avoided. Nobody forced us into it; on the contrary, everyone warned us against it. We did not need to do it to fight terrorism or to protect ourselves from weapons of mass destruction. We had succeeded in getting a very strong resolution out of the Security Council, and as long as the inspectors were on the ground, Saddam Hussein could not do anything that would hurt us. It was our choice to remove him; we set the agenda.

Admittedly, Saddam was a heinous tyrant and it was a good thing to get rid of him. But at what cost? The occupying powers in Iraq serve as a focal point for attracting terrorists and radicalizing Islam. Our soldiers are forced to do police work in full combat gear. They have not been trained for it. They serve as a ready target for all those who want to take potshots at Americans.

The cost of occupation is estimated at a staggering $160

billion for fiscal years 2003–2004, $73 billion for FY 2003 and $87 billion in a supplemental request for 2004 submitted at the last minute in September 2003. But even that is an understatement. Of the $87 billion, only $20 billion is for reconstruction, but the total cost of reconstruction is estimated at $60 billion. For comparison, our entire foreign aid budget for 2002 was $10 billion. Moreover, while it is normal for the United States to put up one-third of the total cost of an international aid project, in this case we will be lucky if a donors' conference will produce more than a few billion dollars from the rest of the world. That will leave the United States holding the bag.*

There are many other tyrants in the world who also need to be removed; this is one of the major unsolved problems of the current world order. Why should we devote all these resources to Iraq? What we have done in Iraq does not solve the problem; on the contrary, it renders a solution more difficult. The American public is liable to turn against military intervention on political grounds just as President Clinton's intervention in Somalia on humanitarian grounds has rendered humanitarian intervention unpopular. Already the United States has been reluctant to get engaged in Liberia, causing unnecessary suffering.

*The donors' conference in Madrid in October 2003 produced pledges of $13 billion from donors other than the United States. This was achieved by smoke and mirrors. For instance, it included $500 million from Iran for financing pilgrimages. More than two-thirds of the pledges were in the form of credits.

We are bogged down in Iraq. Not only are our soldiers' lives in danger, but our military might has also been compromised. Our armed forces have been programmed to bring overwhelming power to bear, as indicated by the code name for the Iraqi invasion: Shock and Awe. They are not trained to perform occupation duties.* Our presence in Iraq was intended to pacify the Middle East; we have achieved the opposite result. Using the invasion of Iraq as a frightening example and Iraq as a military base, we were going to put pressure on neighboring countries; now that we are overextended in Iraq, our ability to project power elsewhere has been greatly reduced.

There is no easy way out. The Bush administration is eager to get the United Nations more involved but is unwilling to make the necessary concessions. President Bush addressed the Security Council in September 2003, but his unrepentant speech was not well received. UN Secretary-General Kofi Annan made it clear that the role of the United Nations had to be clearly defined before he could put his personnel at risk. Resolution 1511 unanimously passed on October 16 did not allay these concerns. In practice the military responsibilities of the occupying powers have to stay with the Coalition, and there will be little support forthcoming from other countries or the United Nations itself. The outlook is grim, but we have

*Wesley Clark, *Winning Modern Wars: Iraq, Terrorism, and the American Empire* (New York: PublicAffairs, 2003).

no alternative to sticking it out and paying the price for our mistake. Eventually a different president with a different attitude toward international cooperation may be more successful in extricating us.

My particular concern is that the debacle in Iraq will prevent future efforts at nation building. I find it unconscionable that the Bush administration is seeking to justify the invasion of Iraq by invoking Saddam's atrocities now that the original grounds cannot be substantiated. We had tolerated Saddam's abuses for many years without doing anything about them. We must find a way to get rid of the likes of Saddam, but the Bush administration's behavior in Iraq renders the task more difficult.

CHAPTER 5

The State of the Union

SINS OF OMISSION

Iraq shows vividly the fallacy of the idea of American supremacy as pursued by the Bush administration. The invasion of Iraq has reduced our ability to pursue the war on terrorism and to maintain our dominant position in the world. That position is for us to lose, and President Bush has taken us a long way in that direction. But Iraq is not the only problem in the world; it is only President Bush who has made it appear so. He is also responsible for all the issues that are *not* being addressed, the lack of progress in international cooperation. The range of unresolved problems is overwhelming.

Africa and, to a lesser extent, Central Asia and South Asia are seething with latent conflicts, but we are not in a position to deal with them properly. We did send some troops to Liberia, but we did so several months too late, after a great deal of avoidable suffering. Presumably this will help to calm the situation in the neighboring countries, but war is still pending between Eritrea and Ethiopia, the problems in Central Africa (Democratic Republic of the Congo, Rwanda, Burundi) are far from settled, and Robert Mugabe is still in power in Zimbabwe. Although the conflict between India and Pakistan seems to have died down, the internal situation in Pakistan remains precarious. Indonesia has been shaken by terrorists, and the rebellion in Aceh continues to cause trouble. In Burma (Myanmar), a sole dictator has replaced the military junta and rearrested the country's democratically elected leader, Aung San Suu Kyi.

One area that is within the power of the Bush administration to affect is the Israel-Palestinian conflict. The outline of an eventual settlement—a return to the 1967 borders with some minor modifications and the abandonment of the Palestinians' right to return to Israel—is known. A roadmap has been published on how to get there. The majority of the population on both sides is yearning for peace, but because of the long and troubled history, no progress can be made without outside pressure. The United States, in cooperation with the European Union, could act as the guarantor of a peace process. So far President Bush has resisted following in the footsteps of President Clinton, yet in retrospect, Clinton's approach was much better. It kept down the bloodshed and came within striking distance of a settlement.

North Korea has created a quandary for the Bush administration. Having denounced the approach taken by the Clinton administration, the present administration cannot now return to this approach. Military action is unthinkable because North Korea could inflict immense damage on South Korea, killing millions before the regime could be destroyed. A blockade is difficult to impose because South Korea may balk in view of its exposed position. The only possible way out is for third parties to provide the economic assistance that the Clinton administration supplied directly. China is eager to play a constructive role. But North Korea is unlikely to agree to give up the nuclear and missile capabilities it has already built up, without bilateral security assurances Bush refuses to give, so that it is difficult to see the basis for an agreement. In the meantime North Korea is going ahead at full speed building nuclear bombs. The situation is worse than it was when President Bush came into office.

Iran is also proceeding with its nuclear program although ostensibly for civilian purposes. Iran is still a member of the Nuclear Non-Proliferation Treaty, but it is getting closer to being able to produce nuclear bombs. The treaty has, in effect, broken down. India and Pakistan refused to sign the NPT and have developed nuclear weapons, and after some initial protests, they have now been accepted as nuclear powers. Japan is considering going nuclear. The nuclear powers, in turn, have done nothing to carry out their obligations under the treaty to undertake effective measures in the direction of nuclear disarmament.*

Public attention is focused on nuclear weapons' falling into the hands of terrorists; the problem of nuclear weapons in the hands of states deserve a lot more consideration. The danger that states will use them is much greater than during the Cold War. Then, there was a MAD balance—Mutually Assured Destruction; now, incentives are in place for countries to graduate from nonnuclear to nuclear status.

During the Cold War the best brains were engaged in studying the problem; now it is much lower on the agenda. The attitude of the Bush administration is particularly disturbing: It is considering introducing tactical nuclear weapons into our arsenal. This will bring much closer the day when we actually employ them. Yet the idea of self-imposed constraints seems alien to the thinking of American supremacists.

*The Nuclear Non-Proliferation Treaty also presents itself as an intermediate step toward a treaty explicitly directed at nuclear disarmament: "Desiring to further the easing of international tension and the strengthening of trust between States in order to facilitate the cessation of the manufacture of nuclear weapons, the liquidation of all their existing stockpiles, and the elimination from national arsenals of nuclear weapons and the means of their delivery pursuant to a Treaty on general and complete disarmament under strict and effective international control . . . " (text available at http://www.state.gov/t/np/trty/16281.htm#treaty).

The situation is not uniformly bleak. The Bush admin-istration has made some positive moves. It has established the Millennium Challenge Account and promised $15 bil-lion for fighting AIDS. Under U.S. pressure, Said Ibrahim was released from jail in Egypt, creating a window of op-portunity for strengthening civil society in that country. James Baker visited Georgia in order to assure that the forthcoming elections will be reasonably free and fair. And there are no doubt many other examples of construc-tive intervention. But on the whole, the United States has become less effective in promoting human rights and the values of open society since President Bush came to power. And no attempt was made to address environmen-tal or social problems; on the contrary, actions already taken were reversed. The pursuit of terrorists is making some progress. They have difficulties in communicating with each other because our electronic surveillance meth-ods are very effective. With all the vigilance, the chances of another major attack on U.S. soil are greatly reduced. But the war on terrorism as pursued by the Bush adminis-tration has actually increased the terrorist threat. Anti-American sentiment is virulent, and as President Bush admits, Iraq has become the central front.

Domestic Policies

I could not possibly do justice to the task of evaluating the Bush administration's domestic policies in the social and environmental spheres. In any case, a book devoted to America's role in the world is not the right place for it. The trends are grim: Poverty has increased, jobs have been lost, and environmental regulation has been atrociously favorable to business interests. I shall confine my remarks to one subject I know something about: the budget deficit.

President Bush came into office with a plan to aggressively cut taxes. It was a bold plan because it so blatantly favored the rich. If the benefits had been more evenly distributed, there would have been no room left for further tax cuts, because afterward, more people would have benefited from an increase in government services than from any further reduction in taxation. In the event, President Bush managed to introduce further tax cuts as a way of stimulating the economy.

The combination of all the tax cuts with a large increase in military spending resulted in a radical shift from a budget surplus of $236 billion in fiscal 2000 to a budget deficit of $375 billion in 2003, with $565 billion in prospect for 2004 before the full bill for Iraq has been presented. This is the biggest swing in history excepting times of war, but then, we are on a war footing as a result of the Bush administration's policies. This suits the administration's agenda because it seeks to squeeze social spending mercilessly.

Karl Rove, the Republicans' master strategist, has resolved to get the economy going before the November 2004 elections in order to avoid a repeat of the elder President Bush's defeat after the first Gulf War in 1992. Federal Reserve Chairman Alan Greenspan is equally determined. He had been blamed for the 1992 defeat, and he does not want to be blamed again. He was proposing a fifty-basis-point cut in the federal funds rate in June 2003, but a less politically motivated Open Market Committee authorized only twenty-five basis points.

The economy is bound to respond to all the stimuli thrown at it. The second half of 2003 will have shown a healthy pickup in economic activity and profits although not in job creation. When the Bush administration claims that the budget deficit is harmless, I have to disagree. Quite apart from the burden that it imposes on future generations—the solvency of our social security system is already in doubt—the budget deficit is bound to affect interest rates. The impact will be felt only after the economy begins to pick up.

We are entering a phase that used to be known as the stop/go economy in the United Kingdom in the late 1950s and early 1960s before its budget was adjusted to the loss of the empire. As soon as the economy accelerated, it had to be slowed down because of the budget deficit. The recent dramatic increase in the U.S. budget deficit practically ensures the same phenomenon: The moment employment begins to pick up, a rise in interest rates will put on the brakes, stifling the two main factors that have kept the economy going: housing and auto sales.

The rise in interest rates has already begun even before unemployment has declined because of a little-discussed and poorly understood structural weakness called *convexity* in the mortgage market. Mortgage issuers, like Fannie Mae, have effectively given the homeowners a free option on interest rates. When interest rates fall, people refinance their mortgages; when rates rise, people hold their mortgages to maturity. The mortgage issuers have to hedge their exposure, and that is what creates convexity. When interest rates rise, holders of mortgage securities balance their portfolios by selling long-dated bonds, and vice versa.

The market in securitized mortgages is enormous, much larger than in government bonds, and convexity makes interest rates much more volatile than they would be otherwise. That is a real flaw in the system, which is liable to cause a dislocation in the bond market similar to the dislocation caused in the stock market in 1987 by so-called portfolio insurance. Combined with the budget deficits, this convexity practically ensures a substantial rise in interest rates once the economy picks up. This will act as a brake, creating a stop/go economy.

Rove hopes that the economy will start going and will not start stopping before the elections in 2004. The chances of that happening are rather slim. Whether he succeeds in making the economy look better at election time or not, we will have to pay a heavy price for the irresponsible fiscal policy of the Bush administration.

Conclusion

All in all, at no other time has America's position declined as dramatically in as short a period as it has since George W. Bush became president. The swing in our international position matches the swing in our budget deficit. Whatever the flaws in the ideology that has guided the Bush administration, the practical results have been nothing short of disastrous.

Conventional wisdom holds that the reelection of President Bush will depend on the economy. I hope that the electorate will reject President Bush for a better reason. The reckless pursuit of American supremacy has put us and the rest of the world in danger. The only way we can extricate ourselves is by rejecting President Bush.

The forthcoming elections provide an excellent opportunity to deflate the bubble of American supremacy. But it is not enough to defeat President Bush. America must also adopt a different vision for its role in the world. The rethinking has to be quite profound. It is not only the supremacist ideology of the New American Century that needs to be rejected. There were shortcomings in the policies followed by the United States prior to September 11; otherwise, they could not have been carried to the extremes that have been reached under the Bush administration. What a more positive vision for America's role in the world entails will be the subject of the second part of this book.

PART II

A Constructive Vision

CHAPTER 6

Improving the World Order

DOMINANT POSITION

The United States is not the only country at the center of the global capitalist system, but it is the most powerful and it is the main driving force behind globalization. The European Union may equal the United States in the size of its population and gross national product, but it is far less united and far less comfortable with globalization.

In military terms, the European Union does not even qualify as a power, because member states make their own decisions. The United States stands head and shoulders above everyone else; its military budget nearly equals the budgets of all other states combined. Not even a combination of states could rival us, because it would be against the

national self-interest of the countries concerned to participate in such a combination. The most recent example was
provided by the Iraq crisis, in which many countries of the
European Union—the United Kingdom, Italy, Spain, Denmark, and the new members from Eastern Europe—lined
up with the United States, not with the other EU states.

Our dominant position imposes a unique responsibility
on us. It is not enough for us to pursue our narrow, national self-interest. We must also concern ourselves, for
our own sake, with the well-being of the rest of the world.
That is because only the United States is in a position to
bring about systemic improvement. Insofar as any nation
is in charge of the current world order, it is the United
States. The United States is not in a position to do anything it wants, as we have recently discovered in Iraq at
our cost, but very little can be done in the way of international cooperation without American leadership or at least
active participation. That is not to suggest that other
countries are exempt from having to concern themselves
with the well-being of the world. Their attitude is not
without consequence, but it is the United States that matters the most. It is the United States that sets the agenda
for the world; other countries have to respond to whatever
policies the United States pursues.

Improving the world order, of course, cannot be the
sole objective of America's foreign policy. Neither can we
confine our attention exclusively to improving our posi-

George Soros

tion within the prevailing world order. Every country has a multiplicity of foreign-policy objectives, which are often at loggerheads with each other. When the interests of humanity conflict with special or national interests, usually it is the latter that prevail. The common interest ought to rank higher than it does at present. The more successful and prosperous the United States is, the more attention it ought to pay to the well-being of the world. It is in our own self-interest that the system we dominate should survive and flourish.

With the advance of technology, humanity has greatly increased its power over nature. Without similar advances in the ability to manage this power, humanity is now fully capable of destroying itself and its environment unless it develops better methods of protecting common interests. It is incumbent on the United States to take the lead in that endeavor. The proliferation of nuclear weapons poses a specific danger, but other threats, particularly environmental, also lurk. Civilizations have been destroyed long before nuclear bombs were invented.

National Interests versus the Common Interest

The prevailing world order has a great unsolved problem: how to protect the common interest in a world consisting of sovereign states that habitually put their own interests ahead of the common interest. Such behavior is clearly visible not only in the Bush administration, which is justly accused of being excessively unilateral, but also in other governments. Within the European Union, member states try to pull the blanket to their side. Within the United Nations, member states are notorious for protecting their self-interests. Inside the organization, they parcel out jobs and positions among themselves; that is one of the factors that renders UN agencies so inefficient. So we are not looking at an aberration but a general rule. As Henry Kissinger puts it, paraphrasing Cardinal Richelieu, states have interests but no principles.*

The problem has no solution, but some responses are better than others. That is not unusual: To be confronted with insoluble problems is the human condition. It would be utopian to try and devise a solution that would do away with sovereign states and replace them with international institutions. Yet a way must be found to reconcile the common interest with the principle of sovereignty. The most promising democratic way is to establish a multilateral system in which all states submit to the same rules and participate in the same arrangements. We could then rely on international public opinion to determine and protect the common interest to a greater extent than today. The task of leading such an effort must fall to the United

*Henry Kissinger, *Diplomacy* (New York: Simon & Schuster, 1995) pp. 58–67.

States, in view of its dominant position. Our position would be reinforced rather than diminished, as long as the United States turns in a superior performance; but it does require the United States to abide by international rules and conventions in the same manner as do other states.

That is not how the Bush administration sees America's role in the world. It has a visceral aversion to all multilateral arrangements. It believes that international relations are purely relations of power, not law, and since America is the most powerful nation, multilateral treaties and institutions impose undue limitations on the exercise of American power. The only form of cooperation the Bush administration can live with is one in which the United States decides and others follow. This attitude has led to the Bush doctrine.

We need to take a radically different approach. We must lead a cooperative effort to improve the world order, because we are the only ones in a position to do so. As both the International Criminal Court and the Kyoto Protocol on Global Warming demonstrate, international arrangements are much less effective when the United States stands aside. Given our dominant position, we have the most to gain from making the prevailing world order function better.

The Global Capitalist System

While political and security arrangements remain firmly based on the sovereignty of states, economic activities have become truly globalized. *Globalization* is an overused term that can be applied in a variety of ways. One could speak of the globalization of information and culture; the spread of television, the Internet, and other forms of communication; and the increased mobility and commercialization of ideas. For the purposes of the present discussion, I shall take globalization to mean the development of global financial markets, the growth of transnational corporations, and their increasing domination over national economies.

Interest rates, exchange rates, and stock prices in various countries are intimately interrelated, and global financial markets exert tremendous influence on economic conditions in every country. Given the decisive role that international financial capital plays in the fortunes of individual countries, it is appropriate to speak of a global capitalist system.

The salient feature of the global capitalist system is that it allows financial capital to move around freely; by contrast, the movement of people remains heavily regulated. Since capital is an essential ingredient of production, individual countries must compete to attract it; this inhibits their ability to tax and regulate it because that would induce capital to move elsewhere.

George Soros

Under the influence of globalization, the character of our economic and social arrangements has undergone a radical transformation: The requirements of attracting international capital take precedence over the fulfillment of other social objectives. I believe that most of the problems that people associate with globalization, including the penetration of market values into areas where they do not traditionally belong, can be attributed to this phenomenon.

Financial capital is even more privileged than capital invested in fixed assets. Financial capital can move about freely and avoid countries where it is subjected to onerous taxes or regulations. In contrast, once a fixed investment has been made, it cannot be easily moved and is thus hostage to whatever regulations the host country imposes. To be sure, multinational corporations enjoy flexibility in transfer pricing and they can exert pressure on host governments through their decisions about future investment, but their flexibility does not compare to the freedom of choice enjoyed by international financial investors.

The range of available investment opportunities open to the latter is also enhanced by their position at the center of the global economy rather than at the periphery of the global capitalist system. Capital is attracted to the major hubs of financial activity and allocated from there. That is why international financial markets play such a dominant role in the world today and why their influence has increased so rapidly.

Global financial markets work like a gigantic circulatory system, sucking up capital into the financial institutions and markets at the center, then pumping it out to the periphery either directly, in the form of credits and portfolio investments, or indirectly through multinational corporations. As long as the circulatory system is vigorous, it overwhelms all local markets. Indeed, most local capital eventually turns international. But the system is subject to breakdowns. Financial crises affect the center and the periphery very differently. When a breakdown endangers the international financial system, action will be taken to protect it. This gives countries at the center a large measure of protection. The same does not apply to countries at the periphery; they may suffer catastrophic consequences.

HISTORICAL PERSPECTIVE

Globalization as defined here is a relatively recent phenomenon that distinguishes the present from fifty or even twenty-five years ago. At the end of World War II, economies were largely national in character, most currencies were not convertible on capital account, international trade was at a low ebb, and both international direct investments in fixed assets and other international financial transactions were practically at a standstill. The Bretton Woods institutions—the International Monetary Fund (IMF) and the World Bank—were set up to make international trade possible in a world devoid of international capital movements. The World Bank was designed to make up for the lack of direct investments, the IMF for the lack of credit to offset imbalances in trade. At that time international capital in less-developed countries was engaged mainly in the exploitation of natural resources, and many of those countries were still under colonial rule. Those that reached independence were more inclined to expropriate any international capital within their reach than to encourage private investment from abroad. For instance, the Anglo-Iranian Oil Company was nationalized in 1951, to be followed by other waves of nationalization and the establishment of the Organization of Petroleum Exporting Countries (OPEC) in 1973. Nationalization of strategic industries was the order of the day in Europe as well.

After World War II, international trade picked up first, followed by direct investment. U.S. firms moved into Europe, then into the rest of the world. Companies originating in other countries eventually caught up with the trend of going international. Many industries—autos, chemicals, computers—came to be dominated by multinational corporations. International financial markets were slower to develop because many currencies were not fully convertible and many countries maintained controls over capital transactions. Capital controls were lifted only gradually; in the United Kingdom they were formally abolished only in 1979.

When I started in the business in London in 1953, financial markets and banks were strictly regulated on a national basis, and a fixed exchange-rate system prevailed with many restrictions on the movement of capital. There was a market in "switch sterling" and "premium dollars" —special exchange rates applicable to capital accounts. After I moved to the United States in 1956, international trade in securities was gradually liberalized. With the formation of the European Common Market, U.S. investors began to buy European securities, but the accounting of the companies concerned and the settlement arrangements left much to be desired; conditions were not very different from some of the emerging markets today, except that the analysts and traders were less skilled. It was the beginning of my financial career: I was a one-eyed king among the blind. As late as 1963 President John F. Kennedy introduced a so-called interest equalization tax on U.S. investors buying foreign stocks, a move that practically put me out of business.

Global financial markets started to emerge in the 1970s. When OPEC was formed, it raised the price of oil; the oil exporters enjoyed sudden, large surpluses, while importing countries had to finance large deficits. It was left to the commercial banks, with behind-the-scenes encouragement from Western governments, to recycle the funds. Eurodollars became popular, and large, offshore markets developed. Governments started to make tax and other concessions to international financial capital to entice it back onshore. Ironically, these measures gave offshore capital even more room to maneuver. The international lending boom ended in a bust in 1982, but by that time, the freedom of movement for financial capital was well established.

Globalization received a big boost in the early 1980s, when Margaret Thatcher and Ronald Reagan came to power with programs intended to remove the state from the economy and to allow the market mechanism to do its work. This meant imposing strict monetary discipline, which had the initial effect of plunging the world into recession and precipitating the international debt crisis of 1982. It took several years for the world economy to recover—in Latin America, they speak of the lost decade—but recover it did. From then on until 1997, the global economy enjoyed a long period of practically uninterrupted expansion.

Then the removal of the currency peg in Thailand touched off a financial crisis that reverberated around the world. Financial markets acted like a wrecking ball knocking over one economy after another. Only the so-called developing countries at the periphery of the global capitalist system were directly affected. When the Russian default threatened the system itself, the financial authorities intervened effectively to prevent a collapse. The economies at the center of the capitalist system—North America and Europe—barely felt a tremor, and international financial markets escaped largely unscathed.

This is not the first time in history that international financial markets have played such a central role. The antecedents of international capitalism go back to the Italian city-states and the Hanseatic League, in which different political entities were linked together by commercial and financial ties. Capitalism became dominant in the nineteenth century and remained so until it was disrupted by World War I. The global regime that prevails today may have some novel features that set it apart from previous incarnations. The speed of communications is one, but it is questionable how novel that is: The advent of railroads, telegraphy, and telephony represented as great an acceleration in the nineteenth century as computer communications do at present. It is true that the information revolution contains unique features, but so did the transportation revolution in the nineteenth century. On the whole, then, the current regime is quite similar to the one that prevailed a hundred years ago, although it is fundamentally different from that which prevailed just fifty years ago.

When did the current phase of global capitalism begin? Was it in the 1970s, when the offshore market in Eurodollars developed? Was it around 1980, when Thatcher and Reagan ascended to power? Or was it in 1989, when the Soviet empire disintegrated and capitalism became truly global? I opt for 1980, because globalization was a market fundamentalist undertaking. The objective of the Reagan administration in the United States and the Thatcher government in the United Kingdom was to reduce the ability of the state to interfere in the economy, and globalization served their purpose well. Other countries had to follow suit in order to attract or retain capital. In the meantime, the trailblazing countries enjoyed a competitive advantage. Moreover, the advantage conferred by the fact that the main financial centers of the world are located in New York and London was permanent. Judged by the criteria of market fundamentalism, globalization has been a highly successful project.

Globalization is indeed a desirable development in many ways. International trade is beneficial to all parties taken together in the sense that the winners could compensate the losers and there would be a surplus left over. Moreover, private enterprise is better at wealth creation than the state. In addition, states have a tendency to abuse their power; globalization offers a degree of individual freedom that no individual state could ensure. Free competition on a global scale has liberated inventive and entrepreneurial talents and accelerated technological innovations. Although it is difficult to prove, globalization probably accelerated economic growth on a global scale. But the sum of gross national products is not an adequate measure of human welfare.

Market fundamentalists recognize the benefits of global financial markets but ignore the shortcomings. They hold that financial markets tend toward equilibrium and produce the optimum allocation of resources. Even if markets are less than perfect, it is considered better to leave the allocation of resources to the markets rather than to interfere with them through national or international regulation.

It is dangerous, however, to place excessive reliance on the market mechanism. Markets are designed to facilitate the free exchange of goods and services among willing participants, but are not capable, on their own, of taking care of collective needs. Nor are they competent to ensure social justice. These "public goods" can only be provided by a political process.

Globalization has severely impaired the capacity of the state to provide public goods for its citizens by interfering with the most convenient and copious source of revenues, namely, the taxation of incomes and profits while reducing or eliminating customs duties at the same time. As a result, the welfare state cannot be preserved in the form in which it was established after World War II. Countries that have overhauled their social security and employment systems—the United States and United Kingdom foremost among them—have flourished economically, while others that have sought to preserve these systems—e.g., France and Germany—have lagged behind.

The dismantling of the welfare state is a relatively new phenomenon whose full effects have not yet been felt. Since the end of World War II, the state's share of gross national product in the industrialized countries taken as a group has almost doubled.* Only after 1980 did the tide turn. Interestingly, the states' share of gross national product has not declined perceptibly since then. What has happened instead is that the taxes on capital and employment have come down while other forms of taxation (particularly on consumption) have continued to ratchet upward. In other words, the burden of taxation has shifted from the owners of capital to the consumers, from the rich to the poor and the middle classes. That is not exactly what had been promised, but one cannot describe it as an unintended consequence, because that was exactly what the market fundamentalists intended.

The balance of advantage has swung so far in favor of financial capital that it is often said that multinational corporations and international financial markets have somehow supplanted the sovereignty of the state. That is a misunderstanding. States retain their sovereignty and wield legal and enforcement authority that no individual or corporation can hope to possess. While markets have gone global,

---

*Dani Rodrik, *Has Globalization Gone Too Far?* (Washington, D.C.: Institute for International Economics, 1997), 49.

political arrangements remain firmly grounded in the sovereignty of states. We do have some international institutions, but they are not allowed to interfere in the internal affairs of states, except to the extent that these states have delegated their sovereignty to an international entity.

The combination of global financial markets and national politics has created a lopsided system designed primarily for the production and exchange of private goods. Collective needs and social justice receive short shrift because the development of the international institutions that would be necessary for their promotion has not kept pace with the development of markets.

There has been a great deal more delegation of sovereignty in economic and financial matters than in other areas. For instance, in the European Union, there is a common market in which the member states have delegated many powers to the European Commission and a European Central Bank is exercising some of the most important prerogatives of the state—the issuance of currency and the control of interest rates, a central factor in the management of an economy. Yet member states retain sovereign rights in foreign policy, defense, and most other fields. Only with the enlargement of the European Union to twenty-five members have further delegations of sovereignty become unavoidable. This discrepancy within the European Union is also mirrored at the level of the more broadly international institutions. Generally speaking, international financial and trade institutions like the IMF, the World Bank, and the World Trade Organization have greater authority and resources than international political institutions, notably the United Nations. This is in keeping with the lopsided nature of the global capitalist system. Globalization has favored the pursuit of profit and the accumulation of private wealth over the provision of public goods.

The disparity between private goods and public goods manifests itself in a number of ways. First, there is a growing inequality between rich and poor, both within countries and among countries. Admittedly, globalization is not a zero-sum game: Its benefits exceed the costs in the sense that the increased wealth produced by globalization could be used to make up for the inequities and other shortcomings of globalization and there would still be some extra wealth left over. The trouble is that the winners do not compensate the losers either within states or between states. The welfare state as we know it has become unsustainable, and international income redistribution is practically nonexistent. Total international assistance amounted to $56.5 billion in 2002.* This amount represents only 0.18% of global GDP.† As a result, the gap between the rich and the poor continues to grow. The richest 1 percent

*United Nations Development Programme, *Human Development Report 2003: Millennium Development Goals: A Pact Among Nations to End Human Poverty* (New York: Oxford University Press, 2003), p. 146.
†International Monetary Fund, "Selected World Aggregates, Annual Data,"

of the world's population receive as much as the poorest 57 percent. Some 1.2 billion people live on less than a dollar a day; 2.8 billion on less than two dollars a day*; over a billion lack access to clean water[†]; 827 million suffer from malnutrition.** These conditions were not necessarily caused by globalization, but globalization has done little to redress them.

Second, countries at the center of the global capitalist system enjoy far too many advantages over countries at the periphery. Perhaps their greatest advantage is that they can borrow in their own currencies. This allows them to engage in counter-cyclical policies, that is, they can lower interest rates and raise government expenditures to fight recessions. The countries at the center are also in control of the IMF and the international financial system. These two factors together give them much greater influence over their own destiny than peripheral countries, which are in a much more dependent position.

Contrary to the tenets of market fundamentalism, financial markets do not tend toward equilibrium; they are crisis prone. Since 1980, there have been a number of dev-

available at http://www.imf.org/external/pubs/ft/weo/2003/01/data/index.htm.
*United Nations Development Programme, *Human Development Report 2003*, 41 n. 3.
[†]United Nations Development Programme, *Human Development Report 2002: Deepening Democracy in a Fragmented World* (New York: Oxford University Press, 2002), 29.
**United Nations Development Programme, *Human Development Report 2003*, 54 n. 3.

astating financial crises, but whenever the center is threatened, the authorities take decisive action in order to protect the system. As a consequence, the devastation is confined to the periphery. This has made countries at the center not only wealthier but also more stable. It has encouraged capitalists in peripheral countries to hold their accumulated wealth at the center. The productive assets of peripheral countries are, in turn, largely owned by foreigners. The ability of local capitalists to expatriate their capital and the influence of multinational corporations reduces the control of peripheral countries over their own destinies and hinders the development of democratic institutions. The detrimental effects are cumulative, and for some peripheral countries, the disadvantages of globalization may exceed the benefits.

The third major disparity is between countries that have good governments and well-functioning democratic institutions on the one hand, and countries with corrupt or repressive regimes or failed states on the other. Economic progress is usually measured in the aggregate, but within the aggregate, there are winners and losers, and the divergence between them is getting wider and wider. While some countries are moving forward, others are moving in the opposite direction. Unfortunately, breakdowns are much more precipitous than positive developments and can undo many years of progress at one stroke. What is worse, one stroke is likely to be followed by another. Armed conflicts, repressive regimes, and financial crises tend to feed on themselves and each other. Some countries seem to be caught in traps of this sort; they form an underclass in the global capitalist system.* Reversing these downward spirals is a major challenge for the world. As things stand now, the principle of sovereignty stands in the way of interfering in the internal affairs of states. The existing international institutions are not up to the tasks of preserving peace, preventing civil strife, and removing recalcitrant dictators.

In *George Soros On Globalization*, I explored the shortcomings of the prevailing world order, but I focused exclusively on its economic and financial aspects. I examined how our existing international financial and trade institutions (IFTIs) could be improved, and I argued that, in addition to their other deficiencies, there was a missing component, namely, better ways of providing international assistance.

I had good reasons for taking this tack. I was concerned that the unwitting alliance between market fundamentalists on the right and antiglobalization activists on the left could undermine or destroy our IFTIs. My concern was triggered by slogans like "WTO, shrink or sink" on the one hand and the negative attitude of the U.S. Congress toward international treaties and institutions on the other. I

*A World Bank team under the direction of Paul Collier has done pathbreaking research on the subject. See Paul Collier et al., *Breaking the Conflict Trap: Civil War and Development Policy* (Washington, D.C.: World Bank and Oxford University Press, 2003).

felt I could lay claim to some expertise in financial markets and I had some practical suggestions to offer. Yet less than two years later, I feel that I have to broaden my analysis and include not only economic and financial considerations but also political and security ones.

I am driven to do this by the way the Bush administration responded to the terrorist attack on September 11. While my primary concern used to be with the excesses of market fundamentalists, I am now much more worried about the excesses of American supremacists. I do not mean to minimize the terrorist threat: The two are intimately interlinked. It is September 11 that has enabled the American supremacists to indulge in excesses and carry the nation with them. It is the Bush administration that is asserting that, after September 11, nothing will ever be the same. And it is the United States that sets the agenda for the world.

In casting the net wider, I shall approach the three major disparities I have identified in the global capitalist system—between public goods and private goods, center and periphery, and good and bad governments—from a different angle. Instead of focusing on the role of IFTIs as I did before, I want to concentrate on the role of states, particularly the United States.

We live in a much more interdependent world than ever before, but our political arrangements are still based on the sovereignty of states. What happens within individual countries is of concern to all other countries. This was true before September 11, but the terrorist attack brought it home as never before. Yet, the principle of sovereignty stands in the way of interfering in the internal affairs of other countries. That is the great unresolved problem of the current world order. The invasion of Iraq was the wrong way to tackle the problem. Is there a better way? That is the question I shall examine in the next chapters.

CHAPTER 7

Sovereignty and Intervention

Sovereignty is a historic concept born of an era when society consisted of rulers and subjects, not citizens. It became the cornerstone of international relations with the Treaty of Westphalia in 1648. After thirty years of religious wars, it was agreed that the ruler had the right to determine the religion of his subjects: *Cuius regio eius religio.* In the French Revolution, the king was overthrown and sovereignty was taken over by the people. It ought to have belonged to the people ever since. In practice, sovereignty was exercised by governments. A dynastic concept of sovereignty was superseded by a national one. Some states are democratic, others are not. There is not much anybody can do about it, because the principle of sovereignty protects repressive regimes from external interference.

Anachronistic or not, sovereignty remains the basis of the current world order. It would be utopian to think otherwise. As we have seen, we live in a lopsided world: The economy is globalized, but political power remains rooted in the sovereignty of states.

This poses two distinct challenges: first, how to intervene in the internal affairs of sovereign states and, second, how to ensure that the intervention serves the common interest. Most existing international institutions—the United Nations foremost among them—are associations of sovereign states that tend to put their national interests ahead of the common interest. Who, then, has the authority to interfere, and on what grounds?

Constructive Intervention

There is a relatively simple solution to the first problem. Offering help does not interfere with the sovereignty of states: They can take it or leave it. Foreign aid and other forms of assistance can serve as effective instruments for improving internal conditions without running afoul of the principle of sovereignty.

Global capitalism has created global markets, and market discipline militates against any form of international assistance. As a result, current international arrangements lack a proper balance between constructive and punitive

George Soros

measures. That is a deficiency of the global capitalist system. Constructive, affirmative actions ought to play a much bigger role. They do not violate the sovereignty of the recipient country, and withdrawing support could serve as a punitive measure that similarly respects the sovereignty of the country concerned.

But foreign aid is only part of the answer. It applies only to countries that are willing to accept it. That leaves the hard part: countries with repressive and corrupt governments that resist external interference. These cases require outside intervention even more than countries that are eager to obtain foreign aid. How can intervention be reconciled with the principle of sovereignty?

People's Sovereignty

The principle of sovereignty needs to be reconsidered. Sovereignty belongs to the people; the people are supposed to delegate it to the government through the electoral process. But not all governments are democratically elected and even democratic governments may abuse the authority thus entrusted to them. If the abuses of power are severe enough and the people are deprived of opportunities to correct them, outside interference is justified. International intervention is often the only lifeline available to the oppressed.

The people's sovereignty is a powerful principle. It is easily understood and accepted. It is deeply rooted in the Enlightenment thinking that inspired the architects of the French Revolution to transfer sovereignty from the king to the people.* In practice, there is much to be gained from going back to the original (revolutionary) idea.† The current world order is built on the sovereignty accrued to the state and its government. By specifying that *sovereignty belongs to the people*, we can penetrate into the nation-state and protect the rights of the people.

The concept of the people's sovereignty is not without its complications. When different ethnic or affinity groups are involved, how do you decide which group is entitled to self-determination? This question created a lot of deficiencies in the peace settlements after World War I. Iraq serves as an example of those deficiencies. But as a general principle, the concept is a valuable one.

THE RESPONSIBILITY TO PROTECT

The rulers of a sovereign state have a responsibility to protect the citizens. When they fail to do so, the responsibility should be transferred to the international commu-

*The same happened in the American Revolution, but in that case, it was a foreign king that was deposed.
†Actually, the idea can be traced back to Marsiglius of Padua in the fourteenth century.

nity. That principle ought to guide the international community in its policies. One of my main objections to the American intervention in Iraq is that it has compromised this principle by substituting American might for international legitimacy.

The principle of *responsibility to protect* has been elaborated by a commission reporting to Kofi Annan, secretary-general of the United Nations.* The summary of its conclusions is well worth quoting at length. I focus particularly on its overarching principles, the explanation of how intervention must be shown to serve the needs of local populations, and the justification for military intervention only as a last resort:

THE RESPONSIBILITY TO PROTECT: CORE PRINCIPLES

I. 1. Basic Principles
   A. State sovereignty implies responsibility, and the primary responsibility for the protection of its people lies with the state itself.
   B. Where a population is suffering serious harm, as a result of internal war, insurgency, repression or state

*UN International Commission on Intervention and State Sovereignty, *The Responsibility to Protect* (Ottawa, Ontario: International Development Research Centre, 2001).

failure, and the state in question is unwilling or unable to halt or avert it, the principle of non-intervention yields to the international responsibility to protect. . . .

2. Elements

The responsibility to protect embraces three specific responsibilities:

A. *The responsibility to prevent:* to address both the root causes and direct causes of internal conflict and other man-made crises putting populations at risk.

B. *The responsibility to react:* to respond to situations of compelling human need with appropriate measures, which may include coercive measures like sanctions and international prosecution, and in extreme cases military intervention.

C. *The responsibility to rebuild:* to provide, particularly after a military intervention, full assistance with recovery, reconstruction and reconciliation, addressing the causes of the harm the intervention was designed to halt or avert.

3. Priorities

A. *Prevention is the single most important dimension of the responsibility to protect:* prevention options should always be exhausted before intervention is contemplated, and more commitment and resources must be devoted to it.

B. The exercise of the responsibility to both prevent

and react should always involve less intrusive and coercive measures being considered before more coercive and intrusive ones are applied.

The Responsibility to Protect:
Principles for Military Intervention

I. 1. The Just Cause Threshold

Military intervention for human protection purposes is
an exceptional and extraordinary measure. To be war-
ranted, there must be serious and irreparable harm occurring to human beings, or imminently likely to occur,
of the following kind:

A. *large scale loss of life*, actual or apprehended, with
genocidal intent or not, which is the product either
of deliberate state action, or state neglect or inability
to act, or a failed state situation; or

B. *large scale 'ethnic cleansing'*, actual or apprehended,
whether carried out by killing, forced expulsion, acts
of terror or rape.

2. The Precautionary Principles

A. *Right intention:* The primary purpose of the intervention, whatever other motives intervening states may
have, must be to halt or avert human suffering. Right
intention is better assured with multilateral operations, clearly supported by regional opinion and the
victims concerned.

B. *Last resort:* Military intervention can only be justified when every non-military option for the prevention or peaceful resolution of the crisis has been explored, with reasonable grounds for believing lesser measures would not have succeeded.

C. *Proportional means:* The scale, duration and intensity of the planned military intervention should be the minimum necessary to secure the defined human protection objective.

D. *Reasonable prospects:* There must be a reasonable chance of success in halting or averting the suffering which has justified the intervention, with the consequences of action not likely to be worse than the consequences of inaction.

3. Right Authority

A. There is no better or more appropriate body than the United Nations Security Council to authorize military intervention for human protection purposes. The task is not to find alternatives to the Security Council as a source of authority, but to make the Security Council work better than it has.

B. Security Council authorization should in all cases be sought prior to any military intervention action being carried out. . . .

C. The Security Council should deal promptly with any request for authority to intervene where there are allegations of large scale loss of human life or ethnic cleansing. . . .

D. The Permanent Five members of the Security Council should agree not to apply their veto power, in matters where their vital state interests are not involved, . . .

E. If the Security Council rejects a proposal or fails to deal with it in a reasonable time, alternative options are:

    I. consideration of the matter by the General Assembly in Emergency Special Session under the "Uniting for Peace" procedure; and

    II. action within area of jurisdiction by regional or sub-regional organizations under Chapter VIII of the Charter, subject to their seeking subsequent authorization from the Security Council.

F. The Security Council should take into account in all its deliberations that, if it fails to discharge its responsibility to protect in conscience-shocking situations crying out for action, concerned states may not rule out other means to meet the gravity and urgency of that situation—and that the stature and credibility of the United Nations may suffer thereby.*

This report provides clear criteria for military intervention, much clearer and more acceptable than the Bush

*Ibid., xi–xiii.

doctrine, but the principles for preventive action—which is identified as the single most important dimension of the responsibility to protect—require further elaboration.

CONFLICT PREVENTION

Conflict prevention cannot start early enough. The earlier it starts, the less costly it is and the better the chances that bloodshed can be avoided. In the case of the former Yugoslavia, outside pressure on Milosevic when he abolished the autonomy of Kosovo in 1990, or at the latest when the Yugoslav navy bombarded Dubrovnik a year later, could have averted the succession of tragedies that befell the region over the next decade.

The Baltic states, particularly Latvia and Estonia, provide a more positive example of the potential for conflict prevention. These states were forcibly integrated into the Soviet Union in 1940, and under Soviet rule, much of the local population was deported and other nationalities brought in. When the Baltics regained their independence in 1991, there was a strong impulse to deny members of these other nationalities the rights of citizenship. Such mistreatment of the sizable Russian populations within these countries could have provided Russia with a compelling excuse for armed intervention. All the makings of armed conflict were present, but the Organization for Security and Cooperation in Europe (OSCE) and the European Union exerted pressure on the Baltic states to guarantee minorities proper legal rights and protections. My foundations devoted to fostering open societies were actively engaged, among others, in giving language instruction and supporting other forms of ethnic reconciliation. A potential crisis was defused, and the Baltics avoided the fate of the Balkans.

The trouble with early crisis prevention is that a crisis that has been averted does not make the headlines. Look at the amount of attention the Balkans have received while the Baltic states stayed below the radar screens. As things stand now, conditions have to deteriorate beyond a certain point before governments are willing to take a firm stand. The point is usually reached when the public has been aroused by gruesome pictures on television, but by then it is too late to prevent a crisis. And as the number of crises multiplies, the public is becoming less responsive, allowing crises to fester longer before outside intervention is considered. The tardiness of the U.S. intervention in Liberia is a case in point.

Since it is hard to predict in the early stages which conflict or grievance will develop into bloodshed, the most effective form of prevention is to reduce the potential for crises to develop. This requires systemic reforms. Such reforms will not eliminate deadly conflicts, but will reduce the probability of their incidence.

We have seen what the iniquities of global capitalism

are: disparities between center and periphery; private goods and public goods; and, most importantly, good governments and bad governments. As the economist Jeffrey Sachs puts it, the two major sources of poverty and misery in the world are bad location and bad government.* By bad government, I mean repressive, corrupt, or inept regimes, failed states, and internal conflicts. There is not much that one can do about bad location, but a lot can be done about bad government. In my view, the most effective way to prevent conflicts is by fostering the development of open societies all over the world. That has been the guiding principle of my foundations after the disintegration of the Soviet empire: It could almost be called the Soros doctrine. The United States would do well to replace the Bush doctrine of preemptive action of a military nature with a doctrine of preventive action of a constructive nature.

*Jeffrey Sachs, "Institutions Matter, but not for Everything," IMF Finance and Development, Vol. 40, No. 2, June 2003. More detailed analysis on geography, governance, and development can be found in John Luke Gallup and Jeffrey D. Sachs with Andrew D. Mellinger, "Geography and Economic Development," in Boris Pleskovic and Joseph E. Stiglitz, eds., *Annual* World Bank Conference on Development Economics 1998 (April), The World Bank: Washington, D.C. Available at: http://www.earthinstitute.columbia.edu/about/director/pubs/sachs060203.pdf, http://www.earthinstitute.columbia.edu/about/director/pubs/paper39.pdf.

George Soros

The Warsaw Declaration

Actually, I have no right to call the promotion of open societies the Soros doctrine. The idea was endorsed in a little-known document, the Warsaw Declaration. This document proclaimed that it is in the interest of *all* democratic countries taken as a group to foster the development of democracy in *all other* countries.*

The declaration was signed by 107 states (a greater number than the number of democracies in the world), including the United States, at a conference held in Warsaw in 2000. The conference was sponsored by Madeleine Albright's State Department. The Warsaw Declaration has remained, however, a piece of paper and would not even have made it into the newspapers if France had not refused to sign it because it had been proposed by the United States.

The Warsaw Declaration deserves more attention than it has received because it establishes a valid basis for intervening in the internal affairs of sovereign states. There are two arguments in its favor. One relates to the people whose sovereignty is abused: They need outside support. Often, outside help is their only lifeline. That is an inspiring argument for people like me, but it leaves governments concerned with national interests largely unmoved. The

*The Warsaw Declaration and related material are available at www.demcoali tion.org.

other argument relates to the security and well-being of the people living in open societies, and it ought to move governments and citizens alike. The world has become increasingly interdependent. What goes on inside individual states—even small, apparently isolated ones like Afghanistan—can impinge on the security of the rest of the world. That was true prior to September 11, but it has become more evident since then. Since failed states; repressive, corrupt, or inept regimes, and internal conflicts pose a danger beyond the borders of the countries concerned, it is in the common interest of all democratic, open societies to foster the development of open societies all over the world.

Promoting democracy is closely connected with economic development, and both are related to national security. It seems far-fetched to argue that we ought to fight terrorism by fostering open societies, yet there is a sound case for this argument. We must, of course, protect ourselves against terrorism by increased vigilance, protective measures, and better intelligence, but we must also address the root causes of discontent. Admittedly, open societies are not devoid of terrorist incidents—the Oklahoma City bombing is a case in point—but they do not feed terrorism on the scale of failed or rogue states.

Terrorism ought not to be the sole or even the main reason for addressing the ills of the current world order. Economic development and the promotion of open societies are worthy objectives on their own merit. There must be something wrong with our values if we need the rise of terrorism to remind us of this fact. Indeed, there is something wrong with the global capitalist system: It relies too heavily on the market mechanism. As we have seen, markets are very efficient in allocating resources among competing private needs, but they are not designed to take care of collective needs, such as the preservation of peace, protection of the environment, social justice, or even the maintenance of the market mechanism itself. Prior to globalization, nation-states were better situated to provide public goods; now there is a greater need for international cooperation. The United States cannot be either the police or the godparent of the world. America needs to work together with other countries. This brings us to the second major unsolved problem of the prevailing world order: how to ensure that external intervention serves the common interest in a world consisting of sovereign states.

The United Nations

In my opinion, *The Responsibility to Protect* expects a little too much from the United Nations. This is not surprising, since the report was expressly responding to a challenge by the secretary-general. Since the United Nations is an association of sovereign states guided by what they perceive to be their national interests, it cannot always be relied on to exercise the responsibility to protect.

The United Nations is the foremost international decision-making entity on security issues but is a very imperfect institution. It has set itself noble goals but is not always able to fulfill them. The noble aspirations are expressed in the preamble of the UN Charter, but the charter itself does not confer either the means or the power to translate them into reality. That is because the preamble is couched in terms of "We the People," but the charter itself is based on the sovereignty of the member states, and it is clear that the interests of states do not necessarily coincide with the interests of the people who inhabit them. Many states are not democratic, and many inhabitants do not have the status of citizens. As a result, the United Nations can do only what its member states allow and enable it to do. It is a useful institution, and it could be made even more useful, but if it is judged by the goals set out in the preamble, it is bound to disappoint. The high expectations attached to the United Nations ought to be scaled down to take into account the limitations inherent in its charter.

The most powerful component of the United Nations is the Security Council because it can override the sovereignty of the member states. The five permanent members of the Security Council have veto rights; when they agree and have the support of the necessary majority of the Council, they can impose their will on the rest of the

George Soros

world. This makes the Security Council, in theory, the most powerful institution on earth. Its decisions have the force of law although the Security Council often lacks the capacity to enforce its decisions. In practice, the five permanent members are rarely able to achieve consensus on the most important issues.

This weakness dates back to the earliest days of the United Nations. No sooner was the organization born than the Cold War rendered it impossible to reach unanimity among the permanent members. After the collapse of the Soviet Union, there was a fleeting moment when the Security Council could have functioned the way it was originally designed, but the Western powers did not rise to the occasion. In the Bosnian crisis, they could not agree among themselves, and in the Rwandan crisis, they failed to act at all. More recently, the advocates of American supremacy have developed an ideological aversion to the Security Council because it gives the other permanent members equal rights.

It would be possible to update the Security Council by revising its membership and voting rights, but that is unlikely to happen because it would require the consent of all the countries concerned. Why should France have the same veto rights as the United States? Would France ever give up its seat on the Security Council? There have been innumerable proposals for reforming the United Nations, but they have all foundered on the unwillingness of sovereign states to sacrifice their national interests for the sake of the common interest.

There is a sharp contrast between the Security Council and the rest of the UN organization. The Security Council can, in theory, override the sovereignty of all states except those that have veto rights; by contrast, the rest of the UN organization is subordinated to the member states, requiring their consent to do anything. This renders it inefficient, cumbersome, and expensive to operate. The General Assembly is a talking shop, and the various agencies are hobbled by the need to accommodate the demands of the member states. The agencies also serve as a patronage preserve for superfluous diplomats and out-of-power politicians.

In recent years, the United Nations has suffered from the negative attitude of its largest and most powerful member. The United States suspended payment of some of its dues for an extended period in the 1990s and has bypassed or de-emphasized the organization in other ways. After September 11, the United States has conspicuously preferred to act without reference to the United Nations. Admittedly, the organization has its limitations, but it could be much more effective if it had the support of the United States. The Bush administration demeans the United Nations as ineffective, but it is the administration's own attitude and behavior that makes it so. If ever there was a self-fulfilling prophecy!

Multilateralism

In advocating a multilateral approach, I am not claiming that the United States should in all circumstances work through the United Nations. Since the organization is so imperfect and rather impervious to reform, there must be times when it is appropriate to go outside the confines of the United Nations. I believe we were justified in intervening in Kosovo without UN authorization, and we would have done better if we had relied on NATO and not the United Nations in Bosnia. But unilateral action that goes against international public opinion cannot be justified, and it can endanger our national security by turning the world against us. That is what the Bush administration has accomplished by its rabid unilateralism. We need a firm basis of legitimacy for our actions. We ought to have developed a broader base of support before we contemplated war in Iraq. This support base should have included not only Europe but also an array of less-developed countries, including some Islamic ones.

The Community of Democracies

The Community of Democracies established by the Warsaw Declaration in 2000 could offer a source of legitimacy for intervening in the internal affairs of nondemocratic states, particularly if the intervention takes a constructive form. At present, the Community of Democracies is an empty shell. It meets biannually—the next meeting will be in Santiago de Chile in March 2005. These are talkfests that result in a communiqué to which nobody pays any attention. It need not be so.

The United States, in cooperation with other democracies, could give the Warsaw Declaration substance. After all, Basket Three of the Helsinki Accords of 1975, reaffirming human rights, also seemed like empty words at the time—otherwise, the Soviet Union would never have signed it. Yet it served as the legal foundation for the Helsinki Committee established by Andrei Sakharov and his colleagues in Moscow, which in turn inspired the formation of Helsinki Watch in New York and spawned a powerful human rights movement. The Warsaw Declaration has the same potential.

If the Community of Democracies came alive, it might also take on a more formal structure. Even now, when the existence of the institution is hardly noticed outside the foreign ministries, countries do care when they are excluded. If membership conferred actual benefits, exclusion could become a valuable instrument for imposing certain standards of behavior.

The Community of Democracies could, for instance, become influential within the United Nations by forming a faction or bloc. At present, membership in the various

UN committees is rotated on a geographical basis. This arrangement could continue, but members of the bloc could commit themselves to vote only for each other, thus excluding nondemocratic countries. No longer could Syria be a member of the Security Council or Libya chair the Human Rights Commission. In contrast to other attempts at reform, this innovation is attainable because membership in a faction is voluntary and the other member states cannot prevent the formation of democratic blocs. The formation of an influential democratic bloc of nations would change the character of the United Nations, making it more effective in influencing the behavior of its members. Repressive regimes would be excluded from active decision making; failed states could be put under the protection of the United Nations. The currently insoluble problem of using the United Nations to interfere in the internal affairs of sovereign states could be on the way to a solution.

The same approach could be taken in the various regional security organizations such as the Organization for Security and Cooperation in Europe (OSCE) and the Organization of American States (OAS). These organizations are already quite influential in resolving local and regional conflicts, but their character and effectiveness vary greatly. The OSCE, perhaps because it was formed when the Soviet empire disintegrated, has a remarkably broad definition of security, very much along the lines advocated here, but it is hampered in its functioning by the fact that it is an association of sovereign states. It could be made more effective if the democratic states put their mind to cooperating more closely. The OAS has also been able to exert some positive influence. It was successful in engineering a democratic regime change in Peru when Alberto Fujimori fled the country, and it managed to contain the crisis in Venezuela when an unsuccessful coup sought to unseat Hugo Chavez. The Association of Southeast Asian Nations (ASEAN) is far less political. It explicitly refuses to pay any attention to the internal politics of its members, but this lack of political involvement ought to be changed. The newly formed African Union presents a particularly serious problem because President Qaddaffi of Libya is one of its main sponsors. There is a latent struggle for influence in Africa between Libya and the West, and that is a major source of instability in the region. Unfortunately, Qaddaffi is willing to spend a lot more money in Africa for political and military purposes than the West is willing to spend.

It will be difficult to change the present state of affairs without a change of heart—and president—in the United States. The West is regarded with great suspicion in the rest of the world, particularly in Africa, the Middle East, and parts of Asia, owing to their colonial histories. This ill will has provided a feeding ground for terrorism and other manifestations of anti-Western, anti-American, and antiglobalization sentiments. It also provides cover for local despots like Robert Mugabe in Zimbabwe or President Islam Karimov of Uzbekistan. That adverse sentiment is not a problem that can be tackled by military means. It requires the rebuilding of trust and genuine cooperation. The United States will have to lean over backward to regain the trust and allegiance of the world.

At present, it would be inappropriate for the United States to try to take on the leadership of the Community of Democracies. There would be just too much resistance to the idea. The United States, under a different president, could demonstrate its change of heart by encouraging the formation of a community of developing democracies, to which the United States and the members of the European Union would *not* belong. This could replace the G77, which is currently operating as a faction within the United Nations. In alliance with the United States and Europe, the community of developing democracies would constitute a governing majority within the United Nations, but they would not necessarily be aligned with the developed democracies on all issues.

The World Trade Organization (WTO) negotiations at Cancun in September 2003 saw the formation of an alliance of twenty-one developing countries on the issue of agricultural protection. The clash between the developed and developing worlds resulted in the breakdown of the Doha Round of trade talks. There is a real danger that this may signal the beginning of the end of globalization: Bilateral deals may supersede multilateral ones. The WTO is well worth preserving, but future negotiations will have to be conducted between equals. At present, the developed countries condescend to the developing ones. For instance, the G8 heads of state invite some other heads of state from the developing world to attend a portion of their meetings. It would be desirable for the heads of state of developing countries to establish their own summit. There could be, for instance, a D6 consisting of six developing countries: Brazil, Mexico, India, Indonesia, Nigeria, and South Africa. The D6 could meet with the G8 as equals. This would be a first step toward reducing the disparity between center and periphery and establishing a more balanced world order.

An Alternative Foreign Policy

An alternative U.S. foreign policy would differ from the present one in much more than being multilateral rather than unilateral. It would involve a radical reordering of our priorities. Instead of devoting the bulk of our budget to military expenditures to implement the Bush doctrine, we would engage in preventive actions of a constructive nature. This would require incomparably smaller budgetary expenditures, leaving room for greater domestic spending within a balanced budget. After all, it would be unacceptable to increase foreign aid without a comparable improvement in social benefits at home.

This has to be a long-term strategy. In the short term, we are bogged down in Iraq and we cannot withdraw without compounding the mistake of invading Iraq in the first place. It would be also inappropriate to balance the budget at a time of job losses. But a president who could articulate a constructive vision for America's role in the world would be better situated to extricate us from Iraq than the one who got us in there.

The constructive actions that would help change America's image would not cost a great deal of money. The United Nations estimates the annual cost of meeting its Millennium Development Goals at $50 billion. I have argued for an annual issue of special drawing rights (SDRs), with the rich nations donating their allotments for international assistance. SDRs are international reserve assets issued by the IMF to its members and convertible into other currencies. Less-developed countries would add their SDRs to their monetary reserves; richer countries (as defined in the IMF transaction plan) would donate their allocations according to certain rules. Less-developed countries would benefit both directly through the addition to their monetary reserves and indirectly from the provision of public goods on a global scale. The $8.75 billion annual cost to the United States is just one-tenth of the 2003 supplemental budget for Iraq. An initiative like this would go a long way toward defusing anti-American and anti-Western sentiments around the world. It would greatly improve our ability to defend ourselves against terrorists and to extricate ourselves from Iraq.

CHAPTER 8

International Assistance

It has been more than thirty years since the Pearson Commission set—and the United Nations endorsed—the target of 0.7 percent of gross domestic product (GDP) for official development assistance from donor countries. Only five countries meet or exceed that target.* In 2000, the U.S. contribution was only 0.1 percent, and total official development assistance reached merely 0.24 percent of the GDP of the developed countries. The United Nations has called for additional expenditures of $50 billion annually to reach the UN Millennium Development Goals. The Bush administration absolutely refuses to accept any numerical targets. It argues that aid should be measured by the outcome, not by the expenditures.

*The five countries exceeding the UN target for development assistance are Denmark, Norway, the Netherlands, Sweden, and Luxembourg.

By contrast, after the end of World War II, the United States embarked on the Marshall Plan, which was very effective. It supported the recovery of the shattered economies of Western Europe and fostered political cooperation; it helped the formation of a democratic Germany and created a strong and lasting alliance between Germany and the United States that has been disrupted only since George W. Bush became president. The Marshall Plan was the precursor of the European Union. In the summer of 1988, I proposed a new kind of Marshall Plan for the Soviet Union at a conference in Potsdam, which was then still in East Germany, and I was literally laughed at.* This shows how far the mood has changed between 1947 and 1988.

DEFICIENCIES OF FOREIGN AID

Foreign aid has become a dirty word because it is believed to be ineffective and often counterproductive. This fits in well with the prevailing market fundamentalist sentiments. Unfortunately, the low esteem in which foreign aid is held is not without foundation.

In my book *George Soros on Globalization*, I identified five main defects in the way foreign aid is currently disbursed:

*"Westeuropa muss Gorbatschows Umgestaltung finanziell unterstützen," *Frankfurter Allgemeine Zeitung*, June 11, 1988.

- First, foreign aid all too frequently serves the interests of the donors, rather than those of the recipients. The provision of aid is often directed by national security interests based on geopolitical considerations, without regard for the level of poverty or the character of the recipient government. Aid to Africa during the Cold War provides some egregious examples. After the fall of the Berlin Wall, West Germany—eager to secure reunification—gave or lent large amounts of money to the Soviet Union, with little regard for how it was spent. Later, Ukraine became a geopolitical pensioner of the West. Bad government is the major cause of poverty; therefore, it would be far better if donors paid more attention to political conditions inside the countries they support.

- A second, related point is that recipients rarely have ownership of development projects, which are designed and implemented by outsiders. When the experts leave, not much remains. Programs that are imported rather than homegrown often do not take root.* The aid-giving

*Paul Collier and David Dollar, *Can the World Cut Poverty in Half? How Policy Reform and Effective Aid Can Meet the International Development Goals*, World Bank Reporting Paper 2403, July 2000, 21 (available at http://econ.worldbank .org/docs/1158.pdf), state bluntly that "the research evidence is that donors have not had a lot of impact on policy (at least not positive impact)." Many evaluations of multilateral aid and the effectiveness of fund conditionality consistently conclude that the higher the degree of local ownership of reforms, the greater the success. An IMF paper prepared for a series of seminars on conditionality concludes, "Policies are not likely to be implemented in a sustainable

countries usually channel aid through their own nation-
als—who also act as a constituency supporting foreign
aid. Even international institutions prefer to send foreign experts rather than build domestic capacity. The experts are accountable to those who pay them. Nobody,
with the exception of my foundation network and more
recently the UN Development Programme (UNDP), is
willing to pay for experts who are accountable to the recipients of aid. As a result, recipients often lack the capacity to absorb aid.

- Third, foreign aid is usually intergovernmental. Recipient governments often act as gatekeepers, diverting
funds to their own purposes. In some cases, aid becomes the main source of support for otherwise unpopular governments.

- Fourth, donors insist on retaining national control over
the aid they provide, and there is not enough coordination among donors. When donors compete to deliver
aid, it is easier for the recipient government to divert
the resources for its own purposes. That was the case in

way unless the authorities accept them as their own and unless the policies command sufficiently broad support within the country." Concerns that "overly per-
vasive conditionality" is undermining ownership have led the IMF to begin to
simplify and reduce conditionality in its programs. See IMF, Department of
Policy Development and Review, "Conditionality in Fund-Supported Programs: Overview," February 20, 2001, para. 14.

Bosnia, where international aid was largely wasted and served to feed local fiefdoms.

- Finally, few recognize that international assistance is a high-risk enterprise. It is much harder to do good than to run an enterprise for profit. That is because there is no single measure of the social benefits, while profits are shown in the bottom line. Yet aid is administered by bureaucrats who have much to lose and little to gain by taking risks. No wonder the results are so lackluster, especially when they are judged by the same standards as other bureaucratic activities and without any allowance for the difficulties involved.

It is all the more remarkable that foreign aid has actually produced some positive results in transition countries—for instance, in helping central banks, financial markets, and the judiciary to function. Many examples show that foreign aid can be very valuable in spite of all its shortcomings. The reputation of foreign aid in the United States is much worse than the reality. Most people in the United States believe that we spend a much larger percentage of our GNP on foreign aid than we do in reality and that the money is largely wasted. Countries like Canada, Sweden, the Netherlands, and the United Kingdom spend a higher percentage of their GNP, and foreign aid has a better image in these countries.

The defects identified could be overcome if the necessary political will could be harnessed. My foundations have been generally able to avoid these problems because they are run by citizens of the recipient countries who believe in the idea of an open society and have what they consider the best interests of their country at heart. The foundations have demonstrated what can be done when aid is guided by the interests of the recipients, not the donors. A government official in a recipient country once called me a stateless statesman, and I am proud of that title. "States have interests but no principles," he told me, referring to Kissinger's dictum. "You have principles but no interests."* That has been my inspiration ever since.

Personal Experience

Readers who know of me only as a financial speculator may be surprised that I have been actively engaged in providing outside assistance to countries in need and I have done it by empowering people inside those countries. I have been at it for more than eighteen years. I set up the first national foundation inside Communist Hungary in 1984 and thereafter followed with national foundations in some thirty-two countries as well as regional and global

*The man who paid me the compliment was Branko Crvenkoski, prime minister of Macedonia.

initiatives. These foundations have been operating on a fairly large scale, with total annual budgets averaging around $450 million for the last decade. Having spent nearly $5 billion over the years, I have personal experience of all the pitfalls that beset foreign aid, but I can also report some remarkable successes.

In Communist Hungary, my foundation became the main source of support for civil society. It cannot claim credit for the collapse of the Communist regime—the main impulse came from the Soviet Union—but it helped to prepare the country for democracy. In Russia, my foundation provided foreign aid that actually reached the people. Our single most successful action was to help some thirty-five thousand leading scientists to survive a hyperinflationary period. My foundations contributed to democratic regime change in Slovakia in 1998, Croatia in 1999, and Yugoslavia in 2000, mobilizing civil society to get rid of Vladimir Meciar, Franko Tudjman, and Slobodan Milosevic, respectively. These are only some of the highlights. The task confronting my foundations was to help in the transition from closed to open societies. Everything needed to be changed at once. The foundations responded by supporting myriad initiatives, none of which was spectacular on its own, but taken together, they added up to something much larger: They laid the groundwork for an open society.

The role the foundations played was greatly dependent on the kind of government that prevailed in the countries where they operated. Where the foundations could work with the government, they were able to achieve much more in the way of systemic transformation. One of the most valuable contributions the foundations could make was to increase the capacity of newly installed democratic governments to absorb foreign aid by enabling them to engage experts of their own choosing (and preferably their own nationality). The transition countries were overrun by experts from international organizations, but these experts were serving their own masters and the governments were capacity-constrained in dealing with them. Where the government was opposed to the work of the foundation, the foundations could play an even more important role: They could keep the flame of freedom and the ideal of open society alive.

In addition to national organizations, my foundations also maintain a number of network-wide programs dealing with specific program areas such as education, media, health, information, culture, the justice system, small and medium size enterprise development, and so on. These programs are operated through the national foundations, but the national foundations are free to decide whether to participate; if they do, they assume ownership of the programs.* The interaction between

---

*About 85 percent of my foundations' money is spent in the beneficiary countries.

By comparison, only 44 percent of the money loaned by International Development Association (IDA) and the World Bank over their existence has been spent in the borrowing countries themselves.

national foundations and network programs creates a matrix that combines local knowledge with professional expertise. The matrix is open ended. National foundations have the discretion to operate outside the confines of network programs; they tend to do so in supporting civil society and culture. Network programs may also work with local institutions other than the national foundations; typically they do so in supporting human rights and independent media.

It would be clearly inappropriate to apply the same methods and criteria in a public undertaking as in a private one. Nevertheless, I believe that these experiments in outside assistance have a direct relevance to the policies that the international community ought to follow. I have been arguing the case ever since I established the foundation network. In the early years, I had remarkably little success in influencing policy. I launched a number of policy initiatives, but they all fell on deaf ears. For instance, in 1992 I proposed that a $10 billion IMF program for Russia should be earmarked for the payment of social security and unemployment benefits. The same money that was given to the government for balance of payments and budgetary support could have also been earmarked to finance a social safety net.* If that had been done, the money would have been broadly distributed instead of

*George Soros, "A Cold-Cash Winter Proposal for Russia," *Wall Street Journal*, November 11, 1992.

disappearing and people in Russia would have seen some concrete evidence of international assistance.

To show that a social safety net could be provided, I embarked on a "first aid program" for Soviet scientists. My proposal for the IMF was not taken seriously, but the International Science Foundation was a roaring success. It selected some thirty-five thousand leading scientists in the former Soviet Union according to very transparent criteria of excellence. The scientists received five hundred dollars each, on which they could survive for a year, because of hyperinflation. It was perhaps the only case in which foreign aid was actually delivered into the hands of the recipients. The recipients—and society at large—have never forgotten it. This demonstrated on a small scale what could have been done on a larger scale. Imagine if all the pensioners of the former Soviet Union had received their pensions and the unemployed had been given unemployment benefits: I am convinced that the political, social, and economic development of Russia and the other successor states would have taken a different course.

Eventually, the foundations established a reputation for effective operations and our approach was emulated by other agencies. Our ability to influence policy has been gradually increasing. In 2002, my foundations, in alliance with other nongovernmental organizations (NGOs), launched the Publish What You Pay campaign. This campaign to force mining and oil companies to disclose their payments to developing countries led the British government to embark on its Extractive Industries Transparency Initiative. We have had an impact on American government spending on AIDS and on the Millennium Challenge Account. In addition, we became involved in a number of specific policy issues in the Balkans, the Caucasus, Moldova, Central Asia, and Southern and Western Africa. With the help of the World Bank, we have also managed to mobilize nine Eastern European countries and the European Union to prepare for a decade of Roma inclusion, 2005–2015, to be launched in 2004. The Roma (Gypsies) constitute the largest underclass in the region.

I have found it difficult to distill general conclusions about better ways of providing international aid from the workings of my foundation network because the network was not the product of conscious design. It grew haphazardly, exploiting opportunities as they presented themselves. The years 1987–1992 were a revolutionary period for the former Soviet empire. I found myself in a unique position: I had a good understanding of revolutionary processes, I had a firm commitment to the concept of open society, and I had substantial financial resources. Many people possessed one or two of these attributes, but nobody else had all three. I could not let a once-in-a-lifetime opportunity pass: I devoted all my energies to the foundations. My spending rose from $3 million in 1987 to more than $300 million a year by 1992. This could not be done in an orderly fashion. We did not have a business plan or performance criteria; for the first few years, we did not even have a budget. Only afterward did we try to introduce order into the chaos.

A NEW APPROACH

A lot of research has been done recently on improving the effectiveness of foreign aid, and a new approach is emerging. It emphasizes the local "ownership" of programs, specific targets, greater accountability, and measurable results. Based on my experience, I concur with the new approach but I think it ought to be pursued much more aggressively. I would like to see greater risk taking, although I realize that a publicly financed effort cannot be as adventurous as a private one. Much more needs to be done to improve the coordination of international assistance.

Aid is a policy tool. It can serve to reinforce regimes that move in the right direction, and withdrawing assistance can discourage or punish those that fail to meet certain standards. At present, foreign aid serves the interests of the donor countries; it ought to be deployed in the interests of the people, as distinct from the rulers, of the recipient countries. That is almost too much to ask for, but it is the principle embodied in the Warsaw Declaration: It is in the interest of all democracies, taken together, to foster democratic development in all other countries. Implementing the principle raises all the well-known problems of cooperation and free riders.*

At present, coordination takes the form of donor conferences, in which all these problems manifest themselves in an aggravated form. I should like to see them replaced by task forces for individual countries. These task forces would devise specific strategies appropriate to the countries concerned and donor agencies would be expected to abide by those strategies. As mentioned earlier, I advocated such a task force for Afghanistan.[†] I am sure that the results would have been better than what has actually transpired. Of course, my suggestion is unrealistic as long as the Bush administration remains in office.

THE MILLENNIUM CHALLENGE ACCOUNT

The record of the Bush administration is not uniformly bad. Under the prodding of the pop star Bono, President Bush has been very forthcoming in fighting HIV/AIDS,

*Robert Axelrod, *The Complexity of Cooperation: Agent-Based Models of Competition and Collaboration* (Princeton: Princeton Studies in Complexity, Princeton University Press, 1997); Robert Axelrod, *The Evolution of Cooperation* (New York: Basic Books, 1984); Anatol Rapoport and Albert M. Chammah, with Carol J. Orwant, *Prisoners' Dilemma: A Study in Conflict and Cooperation* (Ann Arbor: University of Michigan Press, 1965); Mancur Olson, Jr., *The Logic of Collective Action: Public Goods and the Theory of Groups* (Cambridge, MA: Harvard University Press, 1965).
[†]George Soros, "Assembling Afghanistan," *Washington Post*, December 3, 2001.

pledging $15 billion over five years. Bono was able to reach the Bush administration's core constituency because he could quote the Bible better than Jessie Helms. President Bush even pledged $1 billion to the Global Fund for Infectious Diseases on condition that the rest of the world match it two for one—a very reasonable demand. Unfortunately, it is difficult to convert the pledge into actual appropriations because the money is needed for Iraq. The Bush administration proposes to appropriate only $200 million for 2004.

The Millennium Challenge Account is another positive initiative. The United Nations held a Conference on Financing for Development in Monterrey, Mexico, in March 2002. President Bush was attending, and he could not go empty handed. Prior to going, he announced the creation of a Millennium Challenge Account and made a commitment of $5 billion over three years. I was in Monterrey at the time, and it was my privilege to point out that the packaging was deceptive: The commitment amounted to not much more than $1 billion a year over five years. My remarks received a lot of publicity in Mexico. When President Bush arrived, his spokesperson announced that there had been a mistake: The amount would rise to $5 billion a year, three years after 2004. That added up to a lot more than the sum originally promised. It meant that U.S. spending on foreign aid would increase by 50 percent over a five-year period. Of course, the amounts are minuscule in comparison with the cost of the Iraqi invasion.

The Millennium Challenge Account represents a major advance in the way foreign aid is administered. Recipient countries are selected according to transparent criteria. Grant giving follows the "foundation" model that I advocated in my book. Both governmental and nongovernmental organizations may apply. Projects must specify performance criteria.

One of the great merits of the new approach is that it pays much more attention to internal political conditions in the recipient countries than before. Most of the eligibility criteria relate to democratic governance and the absence of corruption. There is also a category called economic freedom, which may serve American business interests more than the interests of the recipient countries, but that aspect of the scheme is only a minor blemish. Emphasizing political as distinct from purely economic criteria constitutes a major improvement. International assistance as it has been traditionally administered has been strangely blind to political conditions. That is because international institutions like the IMF and the World Bank are associations of states that do not want any interference in their internal affairs. As a consequence, international assistance has often served to prop up repressive or corrupt regimes. That is changing now under the influence of the new paradigm, and the Millennium Challenge Account makes the change more explicit.

The main weakness of the Millennium Challenge Account is that it is unilateral. There are provisions for the fund to coordinate its activities with USAID—the federal agency charged with the administration of most aid projects—but there are no arrangements for international cooperation. This unilateralism makes it easier to reintroduce American geopolitical or business interests by the back door, and it makes it more difficult to use the fund as an inducement to poor countries to move in the direction of democracy and open society. One of the reasons that traditional foreign aid has been ineffective is that the recipient government could play off one donor against another. I have seen it happen in Bosnia. The same could happen now.

The Millennium Challenge Account is designed to reinforce countries that are already moving in the right direction; it therefore excludes exactly those countries that are in the throes of escaping from a conflict trap or going through a democratic regime change. This means that the fund addresses only one segment of the range of countries that need assistance. While this may seem at first sight regrettable, there is a positive side to it. Research done by Paul Collier and others shows that foreign aid is more effective in the middle of the decade that follows a conflict or a regime change than during or immediately after the conflict. Historically, aid has come in a rush during the first couple of years of peace and then evaporated.

It is important to demonstrate that foreign aid can produce positive results, and the Millennium Challenge Account is well targeted to do exactly that. Providing assistance to civil society where the government is unfriendly or intervening in conflict situations is a much more risky proposition and requires close international cooperation. Success with the Millennium Challenge Account would improve the image of foreign aid and open the way to increased funding. That will be the time to engage in riskier experiments. I am extremely critical of the Bush administration in general, but I am very supportive of the Millennium Challenge Account. I am eager to protect it from dilution or diversion. Unfortunately, it is already getting shortchanged in the budget process.

The Millennium Challenge Account does not tackle the hard cases: repressive and corrupt governments, civil conflicts, and failed states. That is where the principle of the people's sovereignty can be very useful.

Foreign aid should not flow only through national governments. There is a strong case for supporting local governments and NGOs. Democratic governments should not object if aid is distributed in this fashion; in fact, one would expect them to embrace such organizations. But exactly those governments that do not qualify for official assistance may object to the use of these NGO channels. How are these objections to be handled? I feel very strongly that the more hostile the government, the more important it is to support civil society. If the government objects, there is a prima facie case that the government is violating the people's sovereignty and should be treated accordingly.

That has been the guiding principle in my foundation network. In every country, we set up a local board consisting of citizens devoted to an open society and we channel our support through them. The board takes responsibility for its own decisions. Where it can work with the government, it will do so; where it cannot, it will confine its support to civil society and will resist any attempted interference by the government. Working with the government may be more productive, but working in countries whose government is hostile may be even more rewarding. In such countries it is important to support civil society to keep the flame of freedom alive. By resisting government interference, the foundation may be able to alert the population that the government is abusing its authority. In Meciar's Slovakia, Tudjman's Croatia, and Milosevic's Yugoslavia, the foundations were actively engaged in mobilizing civil society and bringing about democratic regime change.

So far, the foundations have been successful in resisting repression because the governments were loath to be seen cracking down on an organization that was serving the interests of the people. That is what happened in Yugoslavia toward the end of the Milosevic era: The foundation was legally deregistered, but the decision was not enforced and the foundation never stopped functioning. Only in the case of Belarus was the foundation expelled, but it continues to function from the outside, and in many ways, it is more effective than it used to be because only those who really care about open society take the trouble to apply for grants.

Official assistance coming from governments or international organizations ought to follow the same guiding principle: The less democratic the recipient country, the more the aid should flow through nongovernmental civil society. Governments and international organizations are in a much stronger position than a private foundation to resist governmental meddling in assistance directed to NGOs. Even the most repressive regimes seek to maintain the fiction that they have the people's interest at heart. This makes these governments susceptible to diplomatic disapproval. Although external pressure can occasionally be counterproductive—the land issue in Zimbabwe touched a sensitive nerve in the African public and Robert Mugabe managed to withstand the almost unanimous disapproval of the developed world by posing as a warrior against colonial oppression—in most cases it is possible to find a suitable pressure point. For instance, when Egypt put the foremost advocate of democratic reforms, Said Ibrahim, in jail for accepting financial support from abroad, the United States retaliated by freezing any increase in foreign aid until he was released. The pressure worked. In a far-reaching verdict, the Egyptian Court of Cassation not only dismissed the case against him but reaffirmed the freedom of speech and the freedom to receive funds from abroad. This decision has created a window of opportunity for supporting Egyptian NGOs working toward a more open society.

9

People's Sovereignty and Natural Resources

There is another major area where the principle of the people's sovereignty has important implications: revenues from the exploitation of natural resources. The amounts involved are larger than in foreign aid. This makes the subject very interesting, and recent developments are so promising that they deserve a separate chapter.*

The natural resources of a country ought to belong to the people, but the rulers often exploit the resources for their own personal benefit. This violates the sovereignty of the people and calls for external intervention. In fact, there has been a lot of external intervention of a commer-

---

*The following remarks relate to less developed countries, not to countries like the United States, where the institutions of private property are fully developed.

cial nature, but most of it has served to encourage and enable the rulers to violate the sovereignty of the people. Most of the natural resources of less-developed countries are extracted by foreign mining and oil companies—only long after these companies have begun to extract the valuable resources may they be nationalized or national oil or mining companies established. The foreign companies seek to obtain concessions; they care not one hoot for the sovereignty of the people. The companies have to deal with the rulers of the country to obtain their concessions, not with the people. The rulers derive their power from the natural resources they control, not from the people they rule. They have little reason to share the wealth, but every incentive to maintain themselves in power. The companies and the governments of the developed countries tend to support the rulers, not the people. These conditions are not favorable to democratic development, to say the least. A large portion of the political problems in the Middle East and Africa can be ascribed to this cause.

Many countries that are dependent on the exploitation of natural resources have authoritarian and repressive regimes, and many armed conflicts revolve around the control of natural resources. In competing for concessions, no holds are barred.* In Africa, armed insurgents

---

*That is what I was told in a meeting with oil and mining company executives. In the development stage, they are eager to fight corruption because it increases profit margins, but without a concession, there are no profits to protect.

George Soros

can actually borrow money on the promise of future concessions. If you look at Africa, you find that resource-rich countries are just as poor as those that are less well endowed with natural resources, but the latter have more democratic and less corrupt governments. Many of the resource-rich countries—Congo, Angola, Sierra Leone, Liberia, Sudan—have been devastated by civil strife. There are some exceptions, however. Botswana has been both democratic and prosperous, because of the farsightedness of the De Beers mining group and the support of the World Bank, not to mention the local leadership.* But the dominant trend for these countries has been in a negative direction. The possession of natural resources seems to militate against peaceful development. It seems appropriate to speak of a *resource curse.*

New Research

A lot of valuable research has recently been done on the subject. A 2003 book by Paul Collier and others, *Breaking the Conflict Trap*, constitutes a breakthrough.† While focused primarily on the study of armed conflicts and their implications for economic development, the

*De Beers is an excellent example of poacher turned gamekeeper.
†Paul Collier et al., *Breaking the Conflict Trap: Civil War and Development Policy* (Washington, D.C.: World Bank and Oxford University Press, 2003).

book also provides valuable insights into the resource curse.

Collier makes a general point of great importance: Development is not a one-way street. Economic development can be negative or backward as well as positive and forward. Conflict, repression, corruption, or sheer incompetence can destroy the economy. Although obvious, this point has been strangely ignored. Development is measured in terms of aggregates; for instance, the UN Millennium Development Goals are defined in this way.* There is an unspoken assumption that such aggregates are reached by a gradual process of accretion, but that is not the case. The aggregates are made up of positive and negative developments. Moreover, these developments tend to be self-reinforcing in both directions. Negative developments are rare, but they tend to be sharp when they occur; thus they make an important contribution to the aggregates. Collier and his colleagues make a special study of armed conflicts, but civil wars are only one element in a series of interconnected factors: corruption, excessive dependence on natural resources, repression, bad economic policies, ethnic divisions, financial crises, interference from foreign governments, and so on. The authors evaluate the relative weight of each

*The goals call, among other things, for reducing by half the number of people suffering from extreme poverty and hunger, reducing child mortality by two-thirds, and reducing the maternal mortality ratio by three-quarters (United Nations, "UN Millennium Development Goals," available at http://www.un.org/millenniumgoals/).

of the factors by using regression analysis, and they come to the conclusion that natural-resource dependency is a major factor in armed conflicts. The reason is obvious: Natural resources provide both the end and the means for armed conflicts. But civil strife is only one dimension of the resource curse; corruption and repression are other dimensions. Many countries rich in natural resources are caught in a trap of poverty and misery.

The Collier team's practical research has significant theoretical implications. The conflict trap and the resource curse are instances of self-reinforcing processes that contradict the contention of market fundamentalists that allowing people to pursue their self-interest leads to equilibrium and the optimum allocation of resources. Life is full of traps, and markets do not necessarily lead to equilibrium. Success and failure are often self-reinforcing.

Without reversing backward development, a country can make little progress in meeting development goals. Even if the aggregates rise, the improvement is achieved at the cost of greater disparity between the rich and the poor, the free and the oppressed. That is, in fact, happening today, both within countries and internationally.

Helping individuals, groups, and countries to escape from a variety of development traps ought to be recognized as the primary objective of development policies. The very nature of the trap means that the trapped entity usually requires outside assistance to escape. Outside assistance is not indispensable: People have been known to extricate themselves on their own, but outside help can make the task incomparably easier.

This idea is beginning to make headway. People are gradually becoming aware of the resource curse and the conflict trap. Nongovernmental organizations have become involved. A small British NGO, Global Witness, blazed the trail. Its first initiative was to protect the rain forests of Cambodia by closing the Thai-Cambodian border to Khmer Rouge timber exports in May 1995, ending the trade in scarce hardwoods. The resulting loss of revenue played a key role in the demise of that genocidal organization. Then Global Witness turned its attention to the problem of diamonds in Liberia, Sierra Leone, and Angola. The organization's campaign against conflict diamonds led to the Kimberley Process of Certification, which is now being implemented.

In 2002, Global Witness, together with more than sixty groups from around the world, launched Publish What You Pay. As mentioned previously, the goal of the campaign was to force natural-resource companies to disclose their payments to developing countries. I am proud to be associated with Global Witness and the Publish What You Pay campaign.

Publish What You Pay is only the first step in tackling the resource curse. Governments must disclose what they receive, and even more importantly, they must be held ac-

George Soros

countable for the way they use their revenues. That is what Caspian Revenue Watch, which I also support, seeks to accomplish in the oil-rich countries of the Caspian region—notably Azerbaijan and Kazakhstan. The organization aims to build the capacity of civil society, through research, training, and partnerships, to monitor the collection and expenditure of government revenues from the mining and oil sectors.

Some corrupt governments in search of respectability have decided to set up oil funds. For instance, President Nursultan A. Nazarbayev of Kazakhstan was embarrassed by the discovery of a large Swiss bank account over which he had control. To give the account some legitimacy, the money was put into a conservatively managed oil fund imitating the Norwegian model. It is questionable whether that is the best use of the money. Why should a Kazakh oil fund invest in U.S. mortgage bonds instead of creating a mortgage bond market for Kazakhstan?

A 2003 report published by the International Monetary Fund analyzes the way Nigerian oil revenues have been squandered over the years. The report argues that if the revenues were distributed directly to the population, every household would get about $140, representing about 43 percent of current per-capita GDP.* In the case

*Xavier Sala-i-Martin and Arvind Subramanian, "Addressing the Natural Resource Curse: An Illustration from Nigeria," IMF Working Paper 03/139, July 2003, 19, available at http://www.imf.org/external/pubs/ft/wp/2003/wp03139 .pdf. The authors go on to suggest that direct distribution of oil proceeds could

of Nigeria, cash distributions would really make sense because the complicated relationship between federal, state, and local authorities makes it practically impossible to prevent oil revenues from disappearing.

The Chad-Cameroon oil pipeline offers a valuable example of what can be accomplished by greater transparency. The World Bank financed the project only on condition that Chad commit itself to independent monitoring and that the revenues from the pipeline be used for poverty reduction. A stringent supervisory mechanism was put in place with civil society participation, and almost immediately, the Chad government was caught diverting much of a $25 million signature bonus for arms purchases. Most of the money was recovered. There is a clear need to extend the mandate of this oversight mechanism, which, although it has proven its effectiveness, expired when oil began to flow through the pipeline in July 2003.

The Publish What You Pay campaign was welcomed by the British government, and many oil and mining companies also responded positively. British Prime Minister Tony Blair announced an Extractive Industries Transparency Initiative (EITI) at the World Summit on Sustainable Development in Johannesburg in September 2002. The need for greater transparency in the manage-

---

ultimately benefit the quality of Nigerian government institutions. Deprived of a direct source of income, the government would be dependent on, and thus more accountable to, public taxpayers.

ment of resource revenues was endorsed by the G8 declaration at Evian in June 2003. This was followed by a high-level meeting hosted by the U.K. government in London later that month. It was attended by governments, major oil and mining companies, international financial institutions, and representatives of civil society. The overwhelming majority of the fifty-nine participants endorsed the principles of EITI. A few producing countries volunteered to be pilot cases in which the government and all the companies involved would disclose revenues and their use according to templates designed by the U.K. team. The volunteers were East Timor, Ghana, Mozambique, and Sierra Leone, with other important producing countries indicating that they may follow. British Petroleum is taking the initiative of publishing a detailed country-by-country breakdown of revenues and expenditures. Angola, which originally opposed British Petroleum's initiative, has withdrawn its objection. Kazakhstan, which originally opposed the report of the Caspian Revenue Watch, has promised to cooperate with it. Azerbaijan is working with British Petroleum, which is the operator of the largest oil development in the country, to avoid large-scale misappropriation of revenues. Even the U.S. government and the major U.S. oil companies, which at first wanted nothing to do with Publish What You Pay, are now reluctantly joining the parade.

It is too early to declare victory. On the contrary, now

that resource revenue transparency has become politically correct, there is a real danger that everyone will pay lip service to it and carry on as before. It will require the continued engagement of civil society to maintain forward momentum. Civil society in this context includes experts, officials as well as NGOs. The issues are extremely complex, and nobody fully understands what needs to be done to put resource revenues to good use. Nevertheless, there is a growing awareness of the issues, and a resource revenue transparency movement seems to be emerging. The potential is enormous. Resource revenues far exceed foreign aid in volume, and if large-scale corruption were eliminated, several of the most troubled countries could have a more promising future. The movement is on the verge of hitting pay dirt.

Greater transparency and accountability in oil-producing countries is of vital interest to the United States. We are dependent on the Middle East for our oil supplies, and Africa and Central Asia will become increasingly important. After our experience with Saudi Arabia, we ought to realize that it is in our interest that the countries from which the oil comes should have relatively clean and democratic governments. The reluctance of the U.S. government to play a more active role is difficult to understand. Promoting democracy and transparency in oil producing countries offers a constructive alternative to the occupation of Iraq.

CHAPTER **10**

Historical Perspective

The role I envision for the United States—leading co-operative efforts at improving the prevailing world order—is idealistic but not unrealistic. Indeed, it builds on a strong tradition of idealism in American foreign policy. The United States is exceptional among history's great powers in its commitment to the universal principles brilliantly expressed in the Declaration of Independence and reaffirmed in the Atlantic Charter (which was in turn reflected in the Preamble of the UN Charter). Even Henry Kissinger, the apostle of geopolitical realism, acknowledges what he calls "American exceptionalism."* By this he means that the United States comes closer to basing its foreign policy on principles than do most other countries.

*Henry Kissinger, *Diplomacy* (New York: Simon and Schuster, 1995).

In World War II, America fought for the survival of democracy and human rights—although the expression *human rights* was not as popular then as it has become since. America's war aims were avidly supported by many people in Europe, and the United States lived up to its image as the bastion of freedom and democracy. After the war, the United States continued in the same spirit. The alliance with the Soviet Union broke down because the Soviet Union failed to respect the principles of democracy and turned the countries allotted to it by the Yalta agreement into satellites. (Roosevelt's consent to a division of Europe at Yalta remains a dark spot in American history). The Marshall Plan was a bold and generous gesture—if the United States were capable of anything similar today, it would demonstrate the kind of responsible leadership that I am advocating.

Arguably, the Marshall Plan was not as altruistic as it seems. Europe was in danger of falling under Soviet domination, and American industry was badly in need of foreign markets. But the role I am advocating for the United States is based not on altruism but on enlightened self-interest. By that criterion, the Marshall Plan served its purpose well.

George Soros

Two Kinds of Idealism

The Cold War was fought over ideas as well as geopolitical interests—although once the battle was joined, the two became inseparable. Exactly what those ideas were is an open question that remains highly relevant today. I see the Cold War as a struggle between open and closed society—freedom and democracy against totalitarian dictatorship. Others interpret it as a conflict between capitalism and Communism. The disagreement is not trivial. Open society stands for universal principles, equally applicable to all. Capitalism is based on the pursuit of self-interest and is closely associated with geopolitical realism. The two concepts—open society and capitalism—are not too far apart: Open society recognizes property rights and cannot ignore geopolitical realities. Nevertheless, there is a significant difference in attitudes. Which comes first: universal rights and the rule of law or the pursuit of self-interest?

The difference in attitudes was clearly visible in the divisions within the human rights movement during the Cold War. Freedom House was established in 1941 by people who later became known as neoconservatives and who used human rights as a weapon to fight the Soviet Union. Human Rights Watch, or Helsinki Watch, as it was known in the beginning, was formed by liberals in response to the Helsinki Accords of 1975 and criticized the

Soviet Union for its violations of human rights. In the eyes of the first group, *we* were right and *they* were wrong. The second group treated human rights as universal and was perfectly willing to criticize the United States as well as the Soviet Union. Indeed, many members of Human Rights Watch had been previously active in the civil rights movement in the United States. Americas Watch was established as a companion to Helsinki Watch to monitor violations by both sides.

The distinction became even more important after the collapse of the Soviet empire. The capitalist interpretation led to the immediate introduction of a market economy with little thought for capacity building or nation building, as President Bush would call it; the open-society interpretation would have required something akin to the Marshall Plan.

In a similar way, the Declaration of Independence is also open to different interpretations. I regard it as a declaration of the principles of open society with the proviso that they are not self-evident truths but arrangements necessitated by our inherently imperfect understanding. By contrast, Leo Strauss, who supposedly influenced Paul Wolfowitz and other neocons, cottoned on to the first sentence of the declaration and derived, from the idea of self-evident truths, the concept of natural rights. Clearly that concept plays an important role in the ideology of American supremacists, yet I was not even aware of natural rights until I started studying their view of the world. I discovered that the concept had often been used to impose obligations and limit individual choices. As such, it is associated with conservative arguments and papal pronouncements. For instance, it has been used to argue against abortion.

Two such conceptual frameworks—one built on fallibility and the other on natural rights—are like two ships passing in the night.* It is therefore appropriate to distinguish between two kinds of idealism, one based on the concept of open society, the other on natural rights, in addition to the more traditional distinction between idealism and geopolitical realism. The additional distinction is particularly relevant at the present moment in history.†

The Cold War:
Ideas and Interests Aligned

During the Cold War, idealism and realism were easy to reconcile. Whether the ideal was open society or capi-

---

*For example, Leo Strauss and Karl Popper have totally different interpretations of Plato's *Republic*, and although they were contemporaries, they made little or no reference to each other.

†In a way, this three-way division corresponds to the three national security strategies outlined by the Council on Foreign Relations' initiative: Lawrence J. Korb, *A New National Security Strategy in an Age of Terrorists, Tyrants, and Weapons of Mass Destruction* (New York: Council on Foreign Relations Press, 2003).

talism, the Soviet Union was the enemy. In this respect, the United States enjoyed the best of all possible worlds: It could be both superpower and leader of the free world. There were some differences between the liberals on the one hand and the neocons and geopolitical realists on the other, but they were united in their hostility to the Soviet Union.

The most important disagreement related to the choice and treatment of allies. For the realists, the enemy of our enemy was our friend. Jean Kirkpatrick, U.S. ambassador to the United Nations under President Reagan, drew a somewhat contrived division between authoritarian and totalitarian regimes.* The real basis for her distinction was that the authoritarians were our friends and the totalitarians were our enemies. For instance, the United States was quite close to South Africa in spite of its unconscionable apartheid policy. Foreign aid was largely guided by geopolitical considerations and often served to sustain authoritarian regimes.† Human Rights Watch was highly critical of this approach; Freedom House supported it. Bitter battles were fought on other foreign policy issues. There was very active congressional criticism of a Central Intelligence Agency coup against Salvador Allende in

*Jean J. Kirkpatrick, "Dictatorships and Double Standards," *Commentary*, vol. 68, no.5 (November 1979), pp. 34–35.
†The logic of this approach was similar to the formulation enunciated by Franklin D. Roosevelt with regard to Nicaraguan dictator Anastasio Somoza: "He may be a son of a bitch, but he's our son of a bitch."

George Soros

Chile, U.S. covert support for brutal military dictatorships in Brazil and Argentina, and eventually the Contra
war in Nicaragua—all of which the proponents defended
as justified by the need to fight the spread of Communism in
the Western Hemisphere. Nevertheless, for the most part,
U.S. foreign policy had the benefit of bipartisan support,
with the exception of the Vietnam War, which deeply divided the country and left deep scars and bitter memories.

SUPERPOWER VERSUS LEADER
OF THE FREE WORLD

The Cold War ended with the internal collapse of the
Soviet system and the implosion of the Soviet empire.
This was seen as a great victory for the United States, but
the nature of the victory was never properly understood
because the two roles—superpower and leader of the free
world—were fused. Neither was it clear what the free
world stood for: capitalism or open society. Was the collapse brought about by aggressive U.S. pursuit of the
Strategic Defense Initiative (the so-called Star Wars
scheme), the superiority of capitalism, or the yearning for
freedom within the Soviet empire? The response to the
collapse was equally confused.

The demise of the Soviet empire in 1989 and then the
Soviet Union in 1991 offered a historic opportunity to

transform the region into open societies. The Soviet Union and then Russia and the newly independent states needed outside help because open society is a more sophisticated form of social organization than a closed society. In a closed society, there is only one concept of how society should be organized, namely, the authorized version, which is imposed by force. Within open society, citizens are not only allowed but required to think for themselves, and there are institutional arrangements that allow people with differing interests, backgrounds, and opinions to coexist in peace. The Soviet system was probably the most comprehensive form of closed society in human history. It penetrated practically all aspects of existence: political and military as well as economic and intellectual. At its most aggressive, the Soviet system even tried to invade natural science—the agronomist Trofim Lysenko tried to prove, with the help of Marxist ideology, that acquired traits can be inherited.* To make a transition from closed to open society required a revolutionary regime change that could not be accomplished without outside help.

*Lysenko's most famous work centered on efforts to increase Soviet grain harvests. This result was to be achieved by exposing spring wheat to cold weather, thereby creating a strain of wheat able to withstand the Russian winter. Such experiments, and their lasting detrimental effects on Soviet agriculture, landed Lysenko (alongside Josef Mengele) in the "villains" category of *Time* magazine's survey of scientific achievement in the twentieth century. See "Cranks: Trofim D. Lysenko," in "Cranks, Villains, and Unsung Heroes," *Time 100* Web page, available at http://www.time.com/time/time100/scientist/other/unsung3.html.

This insight prompted me to rush in and establish Open Society Foundations in one country after another throughout the former Soviet empire. I realized the importance of the moment. It is characteristic of revolutions that the range of possibilities becomes much wider. Changes normally beyond the realm of possibilities become attainable, and actions taken at that moment tend to set the course for the future. That is why I devoted all my energies to setting up my network of foundations and why I pumped as much money into them as they could absorb.

The open societies of the West lacked the same insight. They did not understand the historic significance of what was happening and carried on their business as usual. They were stuck in the groove of the Cold War, in which two worldviews and two superpowers were confronting each other, and they did not want to believe that the Soviet Union was changing its spots. The idea of intervening in the internal affairs of the Soviet Union in a constructive manner was alien to the prevailing mode of thinking.

When Mikhail Gorbachev came to the United Nations in December 1988 and outlined his "new thinking" about a more cooperative world order, his speech was dismissed as a ruse.* The U.S. government kept on asking for concessions, and when the Soviets granted them, it asked for

*Gorbachev's new thinking originated in the foreign ministry; the other branches of bureaucracy were much less supportive. For instance, all the human rights initiatives came from the foreign ministry, not the interior ministry. That was a major source of his weakness.

more. I remember visiting Robert Zoellick, now U.S. trade representative, then in the State Department. He told me that there was no way the United States could provide any assistance to the Soviet Union as long as the Soviet Union continued to support Fidel Castro in Cuba. When the U.S. government could no longer deny that a profound regime change was taking place, it decided that it was too late to come to the rescue. When Russians begged for assistance, they were treated as beggars. The Russian economist Nikolai Shmelyov told me he spent five hours on a plane with then U.S. Secretary of State James Baker on the way to a ministerial meeting in Jackson Hole, Wyoming, in September 1989, begging him for support to no avail. Gorbachev was left to his own devices.

I have been far less hesitant to engage in such interventions on my own and received a remarkably positive response. A year after setting up a foundation in Moscow in 1987, I proposed an international task force to study the creation of an "open sector" in the Soviet economy. Somewhat to my surprise—I was much less well known then—my proposal was accepted by Soviet officials. The idea was to create a market sector within the command economy, selecting an industry like food processing, which would sell its products to consumers at market rather than command prices—with an appropriate system for transferring pricing from a command economy to a market economy. This open sector could then be gradually enlarged. It soon became evident that the idea was impractical because the command economy was already too diseased to nurture the embryo of a market economy. But even such a hare-brained idea from an insignificant source was supported at the highest level. It is true that I was able to attract Western economists like Wassily Leontief and Romano Prodi to participate from the Western side. Prime Minister Nikolai Ryzhkov ordered the heads of the major Soviet institutions—Gosplan, Gosnab, and so on—to participate.

Later on, I put together a group of Western experts who provided advice to different groups of Russian economists preparing competing economic reform programs. Then I arranged for the authors of the principal Russian proposal for economic reform, the so-called Shatalin Plan, led by Grigory Yavlinsky, to be invited to the 1990 IMF/World Bank meeting in Washington. The plan envisioned splitting up the Soviet Union into its constituent republics and at the same time bringing the newly independent states together in an economic union. Eventually, President Gorbachev decided against it. Had the plan received a more positive endorsement in Washington with the promise of much-needed economic assistance, the disorderly disintegration of the Soviet Union could have been avoided.

When the disintegration of the Soviet Union brought the Cold War to an end, the United States lost the enemy that had allowed it to be both a superpower and the leader of the free world at the same time. The change found us unprepared. We could not decide which of our two roles we liked better. We tried to be both. But the conditions that had made the two roles inseparable no longer prevailed.

During the Cold War, the free world was threatened in its very existence and sought the protection of a superpower. Western democracies banded together in NATO, which was clearly under U.S. domination. But once the threat of Soviet Union invasion had been removed, the primary impulse for Western unity under American leadership disappeared. Other countries became far less motivated to submit to the will of a superpower. As a result, NATO has changed its character. It has become more like a multilateral organization. This became obvious in the Kosovo conflict, when every major combat decision had to go through a cumbersome approval mechanism and the Pentagon was less than wholehearted in its support of the war effort. NATO has lost the appeal that it had held during the Cold War, and the Bush administration came to treat it as just another multinational institution.

Recovering America's Identity

To regain the identity it enjoyed during the Cold War, the United States ought to become the leader of a community of democracies and change its behavior accordingly. It ought to lead by building genuine partnerships and abiding by the rules that it seeks to impose on others. Since peaceful cooperative efforts do not necessarily succeed, the United States would still need to retain its military might, but this strength would serve to protect a just world order and would be seen as such by the rest of the world.

This vision goes against the grain of the Bush administration's ideology, which I have described as a crude form of social Darwinism: the survival of the fittest as determined by competition, not cooperation. The Cold War fitted well into that paradigm. It was a competition between two superpowers and two worldviews—one based on free competition and the other on the promise of social justice to be achieved by central planning. The 2000 foreign policy platform on which then Governor Bush was elected president sought to recreate the happy days of the Cold War, but those days are over. Our identity has to be built on different premises.

The failure of the central planning model did not prove the validity of the free enterprise model, although that is what those who saw the Cold War as a contest between capitalism and socialism believe. There is a better way of looking at the world. It is based on the postulate of radical fallibility, according to which *all* our constructs are flawed in one way or another. Specifically, both models—Communism and free enterprise, or market fundamentalism, as I have rechristened it—are deficient; the deficiency in each one can be cured only by taking some elements from the other. There can be no doubt that the Communist model turned out to be inferior to the free enterprise one. But that is only because the free enterprise model has been pursued in a less dogmatic, extremist way than the Communist one. Market economies are characterized by large doses of regulation and other forms of social intervention, not by the untrammeled pursuit of self-interest.

In my opinion it is more appropriate to attribute the victory of the West to the fact that it is an open society, whereas the Soviet empire was a closed one. My way of looking at the world, however, is not widely accepted. Friedrich Hayek, the apostle of free enterprise, has been much more influential than Karl Popper, the philosopher of open society.*

Since the election of Ronald Reagan in the United States and Margaret Thatcher in the United Kingdom, market fundamentalism has become the dominant creed in the Western world. The mentality that had inspired the New Deal, the United Nations, and the Marshall Plan seems to have lost its ability to generate new ideas that could be turned into reality. Liberalism is not banished—we are not a closed society—but it has become a political

*Hayek's most famous work is *The Road to Serfdom* (Chicago: University of Chicago Press, 1944).

liability instead of a rallying cry. Even the political left, President Clinton in the United States and Tony Blair's New Labour in the United Kingdom, accepted some of the tenets of market fundamentalism. They were looking for a third way that avoids the excesses of both socialism and free enterprise capitalism. Unfortunately, the third way lacked the coherence and clarity of the other two viewpoints and never gained much traction. I believe the concepts of reflexivity, radical fallibility, and open society could serve as the basis of a coherent worldview that could give new life to old-fashioned liberalism.

President Clinton came into office without any great appreciation of foreign policy issues. He had a domestic agenda, and he looked to his national security adviser, Anthony Lake, to keep international crises from taking up too much of his time and energy. The president failed to appreciate the historic significance of the ending of the Cold War, and he was more concerned with enhancing America's competitiveness than with changing the world order. His perspective evolved with the passage of time. He came to realize that an American president has much more power and influence on the international scene than in domestic affairs. He became personally involved in Northern Ireland and in the Israeli-Palestinian conflict. Acting as a conciliator suited his personality, and he made great strides in bringing both conflicts to a peaceful resolution. In Northern Ireland, the peace process continues, although it is not yet complete. In Israel, genuine peace and reconciliation were within reach, when an Israeli extremist murdered Prime Minister Rabin in order to prevent it from happening. President Clinton persisted to the very end, but success never again came as close as it had been when Yitzhak Rabin was killed. Eventually, President Clinton did develop a coherent vision on foreign policy, but by then the historic opportunity presented by the collapse of the Soviet system had been lost.

It is against this background that the Project for the New American Century was formed in 1997. It proposed a muscular foreign policy, including the invasion of Iraq, that stands in stark contrast to the one I am advocating here. Members of that project became influential in the present Bush administration and came to dominate it after September 11. They have prevailed to such an extent that the idea of America as the leader of a community of democracies sounds quite utopian. Yet it is they who are carrying an unrealistic and unattractive idea—military supremacy—to extremes. The idea of introducing democracy by military means is certainly more unrealistic than doing it through cooperative and constructive measures.

Of course, my vision of responsible American leadership is *not* diametrically opposed to the policies adopted by the advocates of American supremacy. Both viewpoints agree that the United States cannot avoid intervening in the internal affairs of other countries, but I claim that we

George Soros

must do so only on legitimate grounds. The Bush doctrine cannot be accepted by the rest of the world as legitimate. That is why I consider the policies of the Bush administration so harmful. They disbar America from becoming the champion of a community of democracies even before it has decided to assume that role. As I can testify on the basis of personal experience, fostering open societies is difficult even with the best of intentions. It becomes next to impossible when America is seen as pursuing its self-interest. We have lost the moral high ground for advocating a better world order and universal human rights. We can regain it only by rejecting President Bush when he stands for reelection in 2004 and by adopting a more benevolent role in the world.

COLLECTIVE SECURITY

The American public is currently preoccupied with issues of security, and rightly so. The terrorist threat is real, and the prospect of chemical, biological, or even nuclear weapons falling into the hands of terrorists cannot be dismissed.

The right frame in which to think about security is collective security. Neither nuclear proliferation nor international terrorism can be successfully addressed without international cooperation. It is incumbent on us, as the dominant power, to take the lead. Terrorism and weapons of mass destruction have become threats to our national security precisely because we occupy such a dominant position. The right way to respond is by strengthening our collective security arrangements. Our definition of collective security ought to be broad enough to include the kind of constructive, affirmative actions described earlier. The world is looking to us for that kind of leadership. We have provided it in the past, and one of the main reasons for such strong anti-American feelings in the world today is that we are not providing it at present.

While collective security arrangements need to be strengthened, it would be going too far to replace national security by international security. Two considerations render this idea unrealistic. One is that the American public would never stand for it. There is a deep-seated aversion to relying on international treaties and organizations. Admittedly, the current negative attitude is excessive. It has been fostered by American-supremacy advocates, who have been very successful in influencing public opinion. A different leadership could influence public opinion in the opposite direction. Even so, it would be dangerous to go too far in subordinating our national security interests to international institutions because of the second consideration.

International arrangements involve sovereign states. States are guided by their own interests; how can we then entrust our security to them? It follows from the postulate of radical fallibility that no international arrangement is foolproof. There is always a possibility that one of the participants will be successful in evading its provisions, and in that case, we must be able to rely on our own capacity to defend ourselves. The danger of cheating is enhanced by the fact that other participants are less democratic and less open than we are. Given that danger, we are also liable to cheat. Indeed, we have much greater chemical and biological weapons capabilities than any other state.

It would be a mistake to juxtapose an uncritical multilateralism and the rampant unilateralism of the Bush administration. Not only would this approach lose in the beauty contest of the elections, but it would also fail to protect our national security. After the collapse of the Soviet empire and even more after the terrorist attack on September 11, the security threats that confront us have a very different character than before. We are not threatened by the conventional weapons of any state or combination of states. We enjoy an unquestioned superiority as the sole surviving superpower, and we could maintain that superiority with much less expenditure than we currently devote to it. At present we spend almost as much on defense as do all the other countries in the world combined. We are way ahead of them in technology. Naturally they try to catch up with us the best they can, so we keep on pushing ahead on technology in order to maintain our superiority. This is an arms race between unequals that could be slowed down by international agreement. The agreement could be rigorously monitored, and the race could be resumed if there were any indications of cheating. We are in a position to dictate the terms that would satisfy us. We are prevented from doing so only by our own attitude: Nothing would satisfy us, because under the influence of extremists, we are opposed to the process.

CHAPTER 11

The Bubble of
American Supremacy

It may be surmised from the closing remarks of the last chapter that I have become rather rabid in my political views. This is a novel experience for me. I used to be rather balanced between the two main parties, seeing some good and some bad in each and leaning only slightly toward the Democrats. Even today, I remain rather even-handed by finding much to criticize in the leadership of the Democratic Party. Certainly I did not use to consider it a matter of life and death which party won the elections. I do now.

I attribute this change not to some sudden quirk in my character but to a qualitative shift in the role that the United States plays in the world. I believe we have left near-equilibrium conditions behind and entered far-from-equilibrium territory.

To explain what I mean by this statement, I must invoke a theory I developed in connection with the stock market. I believe something akin to a boom-bust process, or bubble, is occurring now in connection with the Bush administration's pursuit of American supremacy. I realize that comparing the present situation to a stock market bubble is a flight of fancy, a fertile fallacy, but it is worth pursuing because it casts new light on the predicament in which we find ourselves. We are caught in a quagmire in Iraq. How could that happen? The comparison with a boom-bust process helps to explain it.

The important thing to understand about stock market bubbles is that they do not grow out of thin air. They have a solid basis in reality, but reality is distorted in the participants' minds by a misconception. As I explain at greater length in the appendix, there is an inherent discrepancy between what people think and the actual state of affairs. Normally the discrepancy is kept within bounds by a self-correcting process: People notice that outcomes fail to correspond to expectations and adjust their expectations accordingly. These are what I call near-equilibrium conditions. There are occasions, however, when a trend that manifests itself in reality is reinforced by a bias or misconception prevailing in the market, or vice versa. A boom-bust process gets under way in which both the prevailing interpretation *and reality itself* are propelled into far-from-equilibrium territory.

Eventually the gap between reality and its false interpretation becomes unsustainable and the bubble bursts. That is what happened in the case of information technology. The technological advances were real, but their importance was exaggerated. Initially, the exaggeration accelerated the innovations, but eventually, the self-reinforcing process became unsustainable. In that instance, the boom was sustained longer and the reversal came later than I and many other so-called experts anticipated. The bust was correspondingly more severe.

Exactly when the boom-bust process transgresses normalcy and enters far-from-equilibrium territory can be established only in retrospect. During the self-reinforcing phase, market participants are carried away by the prevailing bias and fail to notice a growing discrepancy between their beliefs and reality. The misconceptions may be tested, and if the trend survives the test, the misconceptions are reinforced. This widens the gap and sets the stage for an eventual reversal. Although this course of events seems to have an inexorable quality about it, a boom-bust process can be aborted at any stage and the adverse effects reduced or avoided altogether. Few bubbles reach the extremes of the information technology boom that ended in 2000. The sooner the process is aborted, the better.

In my view, the Bush administration's quest for American supremacy qualifies as a bubble. There is an underlying reality: The United States does occupy a dominant role in the world. There is also a prevailing bias, a misinterpretation of the underlying reality. I have described it as a crude form of social Darwinism that regards life as a struggle for survival in which the survival of the fittest is determined by competition, not cooperation. In the economy, the competition is between enterprises; in international relations, between states. To date, America has clearly emerged as the fittest. There has been a reflexive interplay between the prevailing bias and the underlying reality, a benign circle that has reinforced both. The distortion of reality became evident only when the election of President Bush brought into power a group of ideologues who believed in the pursuit of American supremacy by military means. That is when the pursuit of self-interest was carried too far. Until then the self-reinforcing, self-correcting process had stayed well within normal bounds. It was the terrorist attack of September 11 that allowed the advocates of American supremacy to carry the nation behind them, and it was with the invasion of Iraq that we entered far-from-equilibrium territory.

It is one thing to give commercial enterprise free play, but quite another to unleash military power. There has always been a connection between business and the military, and it has always been suspect. President Eisenhower spoke of the military-industrial complex. The nexus between big business and the military can corrupt both. Historically the United States has been relatively free of this influence because it had kept its armed forces small; only after World War II did conditions change, and President Eisenhower was astute enough to warn against the danger. In other countries the connection between big business and the military has been much more pronounced. It could be observed in Imperial Germany and Japan and was at the root of fascism.

As discussed previously, the neocons behind the Project for the New American Century advocated greater military spending, and many of them were associated with the defense and oil industries. For instance, Richard Perle, who received no salary as head of the Defense Policy Board, made a lot of money as a corporate consultant. Dick Cheney was president of Halliburton before he became vice president, and Halliburton's lucrative contracts in Iraq are well known. I do not say that the neoconservative ideology was based on monetary interests—I am no neo-Marxist—but there is an undeniable two-way, reflexive connection.

Until recently the reflexive connection stayed well within the bounds of normalcy, as demonstrated by the lack of progress in implementing the neoconservative agenda prior to September 11. In spite of a determination to introduce discontinuity into American foreign policy—anything but Clinton—Colin Powell at the State Department was able to maintain a large degree of continuity.

Then came the tragedy of September 11, and that is when the process entered far-from-equilibrium territory. As I hope to have shown, it was not so much the terrorist attacks themselves that created an abnormal situation but the Bush administration's response to them. President Bush declared war on terrorism, and by linking terrorism with weapons of mass destruction, he gained a mandate for invading Iraq. The occupation forces of Iraq, in turn, provided a suitable target for terrorists, and we have become snared in a quagmire.

The public did not realize that declaring war on terrorism and attacking Iraq was not the appropriate response. Even today, many people believe that September 11 justifies behavior that would be unacceptable in normal times. The ideologues of American supremacy and President Bush personally never cease to remind us that September 11 changed the world. It is only as the untoward consequences of the invasion of Iraq become apparent that people are beginning to realize that something has gone woefully wrong.

We have fallen into a trap. Traps work by getting people or animals enmeshed in them; cool heads are needed to extricate oneself. The motivation of the suicide bombers seemed incomprehensible at the time of the attack; as we look back now, a light begins to dawn: They wanted us to react the way we did. Perhaps they understood us better than we understand ourselves.

As a proponent of radical fallibility, I am reluctant to ascribe too much foresight to anyone; yet in retrospect I can discern the vague outlines of an imaginary master plan conceived by an evil genius called Bin Laden. From his perspective our civilization is degenerate. It is rich and powerful but devoid of true faith. It needs to be destroyed for the faith to prevail. The only way to destroy it is by exploiting its weakness: the fear of death. It will respond to a terrorist attack by lashing out against an unseen enemy. Since the perpetrators remain invisible, the instinctive reaction will claim innocent victims. The victims will be Muslim, and Islam will be radicalized, provoking a general confrontation between Islam and the West. Although the West enjoys material superiority, Islam will prevail because it has a major competitive advantage: It is not afraid of death.

Events so far have lived up to this putative Bin Laden's wildest expectations. The twin towers of the World Trade Center actually collapsed, making the attack more spectacular than could have been imagined. And President Bush responded by declaring war on terrorism. The real Bin Laden clearly expected a counterstrike in Afghanistan; that is why he had Ahmed Shah Massoud, the only commander capable of mounting an effective campaign against the Taliban, assassinated two days before September 11. The invasion of Iraq was an unexpected gift. American soldiers on Arabian soil are serving as a magnet, attracting al Qaeda–trained terrorists from all over the world. Sleeper cells are coming alive. Around three thousand people with al Qaeda connections are said to have disappeared from Saudi Arabia. Some of them must be active in Iraq. President Bush is right in saying that Iraq has become the central front in the war on terror. Wittingly or unwittingly, he has played right into the hands of the terrorists.

I have been arguing that while the public has reacted instinctively, the promoters of American supremacy surrounding President Bush had a master plan of their own. They brought the plan with them when they came into office, and they adapted it to the circumstances when the terrorists struck. In effect they exploited the instinctive reaction of the public for their own purposes. But they did not anticipate the untoward results. Judged by its own criteria, the Bush administration's pursuit of American supremacy has been a dismal failure.

The two master plans have something in common with each other and with a stock market bubble: They are initially self-reinforcing, but eventually are bound to be self-defeating because they are built on a misinterpretation of reality. This is borne out by a closer consideration of the master plans themselves. We have no difficulty in seeing the absurdity of al Qaeda's master plan of preserving the purity of Islam through terrorism, although we are more inclined to call it evil rather than just false. And rightly so.

What can be worse than killing innocent people in the name of religion?

We may have more difficulty in perceiving the absurdity of pursuing American supremacy through military means, because we have learned to rely on military power and we feel the need for it particularly strongly when our very existence is threatened. We do not think of ourselves as being guided by an ideology; we consider ourselves much too pragmatic for that. Yet ideology has come to play an abnormally large part in deciding government policy, and the discrepancy between perceptions and the actual state of affairs has also grown abnormally wide. This could have happened only by a self-reinforcing process that gathered strength gradually over the years.

Indeed, that is what happened. Once market fundamentalism allied itself with religious fundamentalism it managed to capture the Republican Party. The social Darwinist ideology was reinforced first by the success of globalization, then by the collapse of the Soviet system. It is only with the election of George W. Bush that the pragmatism of geopolitical realists yielded to the revolutionary zeal of the advocates of American supremacy, and it is only after September 11 that the supremacists gained the upper hand.

We should not push the analogy with a stock market bubble too far. Comparing the pursuit of American supremacy to a stock market bubble is an imperfect fit. If we treat it as a fertile fallacy, however, it can provide some valuable insights.

In the early stages of the process, the participants in a bubble do not see the absurdity of their convictions; on the contrary, reality seems to confirm their perceptions. Only at a later stage does the divergence between expectations and the actual course of events become apparent. Then there is a moment of truth followed by a reversal. When the reversal occurs, it becomes self-reinforcing in the opposite direction, and depending on how far the bubble was inflated, it can cause a lot of damage.

The important thing to remember about a bubble is that there is nothing preordained about it. Boom-bust processes can be aborted at any time, and the sooner it happens the less harm they do. There are random fluctuations in stock prices every day, and they do no harm. It is only when critical thinking is suspended or suppressed that the reflexive interaction between reality and its interpretation can get out of hand. That is what happened in the aftermath of September 11.

Where are we in this reflexive process? We stand either at the moment of truth or at a testing point that, if it is successfully overcome, will reinforce the trend. We shall not know which of these alternative applies until the presidential election.

The quagmire in Iraq ought to serve as the moment of truth. Whatever the justification for removing Saddam

Hussein, there can be no doubt that we invaded Iraq on false pretenses. Wittingly or unwittingly, President Bush deceived the American public and Congress and rode roughshod over the opinions of our allies. The gap between the administration's expectations and the actual state of affairs could not be wider. The fallacy in waging war on terrorism has been demonstrated on the ground in Iraq. Our soldiers have been forced to do police duty in combat gear, and they are being killed. We have put at risk not only our soldiers' lives but the combat readiness of our armed forces.* We are overstretched and our ability to project our power has been compromised. Yet there are more places where we need to project our power than ever before. North Korea is openly building nuclear weapons; Iran is doing so clandestinely. The Taliban is regrouping in the Pushtun areas of Afghanistan. The costs of occupation and the prospect of permanent war are weighing on our economy, and we are failing to address many festering problems both at home and globally. If we ever needed proof that the neocon's dream of American supremacy is misconceived, the Iraqi quagmire has provided it.

Unfortunately, al Qaeda has not yet reached the moment of truth. As a result of our reaction to September 11, its master plan is still in the self-reinforcing phase. Far from reducing the terrorist threat, the war on terrorism

*For a cogent analysis, see Wesley Clark, *Winning Modern Wars: Iraq, Terrorism, and the American Empire* (New York: PublicAffairs, 2003).

has actually increased it. We find ourselves trapped in Iraq, and it will be difficult to extricate ourselves. Withdrawing from Iraq is not an option: It would hand victory to the terrorists and do irreparable damage to our standing in the world. Yet the clamor for it is bound to rise. This could lead to a catastrophic reversal, similar to what happened in Vietnam.

Where do we go from here? As I keep insisting, history is not predetermined. I can see a number of scenarios. One is that the Bush administration toughs it out and actually manages to stabilize the situation in Iraq. Another is that the Bush administration recognizes its mistakes and tries to correct them by jettisoning the ideologues of American supremacy ensconced in the Defense Department. The actual course of events is likely to fall between these two extremes. President Bush will try to muddle through by getting both the Iraqis and the United Nations more involved. According to form, elections are not decided on foreign policy issues. Afghanistan is already off the radar screen; if Iraq can be brought under wraps and the economy shows some signs of improvement, President Bush can hope to be reelected. He can then learn from the mistakes of his first term and revert to the continuity that Colin Powell at the State Department sought to preserve.

I do not think this scenario is realistic. We have moved too deeply into far-from-equilibrium territory to return to the status quo. America's standing in the world has suffered too much damage, and opposition to the United States has gained too much momentum, not only in Iraq but worldwide. All the other problems of global capitalism that the Bush administration shunted aside will also continue to intrude.

I favor a third scenario, namely, a profound reconsideration of America's role in the world along the lines sketched out in this book. That will require not only the rejection of President Bush but the adoption of a more positive vision for America. It will not be easy to convince the world that we have changed our spots—remember how Gorbachev failed to persuade us?—but we must make the effort if we want to escape from a vicious circle of escalating violence.

Epilogue

While I was engaged in writing this book—June to October 2003—events have followed the trajectory of a typical boom-bust process. It is now possible to assert that the aftermath of the Iraq invasion was the moment of truth, not a successful test that reinforces a prevailing trend. The Bush administration's pursuit of American supremacy can now be seen for what it is: a dangerous aberration. The tide is turning. People who have lined up behind the president after September 11 are beginning to realize that they have been misled. Their unquestioning allegiance is turning to anger. President Bush's approval rating is hovering around 50 percent, but it is likely to sink as low as it has been high before the process is complete. Guided by my boom-bust model, I am confident that he will be rejected in 2004—subject to all the reservations that need to be applied to that model.*

It is all the more important to remember the main message of this book: It is not enough to defeat President Bush at the polls; we must repudiate the Bush doctrine and adopt a more enlightened vision of America's role in the world. If the presidency of George W. Bush was an aberration, we must learn something from it. An open society makes progress by trial and error. The setback we have suffered ought to lead us to follow more cooperative and constructive policies.

---

*I have made an unconditional prediction once before, in 1997, when I predicted the imminent collapse of the global capitalist system. Later I had to eat my words. On this occasion, I shall do everything I can to ensure that the inevitable actually happens.

Appendix:
My Conceptual Framework

Reflexivity

My starting point is the insight that our understanding of the world in which we live is fundamentally flawed. Stated so directly, this observation sounds trite; only when its implications are fully digested does it become an insight.

When I say that our understanding of the world in which we live is inherently imperfect, I refer primarily to social situations in which we participate, as distinct from natural phenomena that occur independently of what we think, although it also extends to a broad understanding of reality as a whole, the traditional subject of philosophical speculation.

Participation interferes with our ability to attain knowledge. Knowledge requires true statements, and true statements must correspond to the facts. The facts have to be independent of the statements that refer to them if the facts are to serve as a criterion by which the truth or validity of the statements can be judged. Rivers flow downstream, whatever anybody says. But situations that have thinking participants do not consist exclusively of such facts; they also include events that are influenced by the participants' thinking. Whether you are my enemy depends a great deal on what I say and do.

As thinking participants, we can influence the situation in which we participate; therefore, the situation cannot serve as an independent criterion for judging the validity of our interpretation. Even if our thoughts or statements manage to correspond to the facts, the correspondence does not vouch for their truth, because it may have been brought about by our ability to influence the situation rather than by our ability to observe the truth. In the absence of an independent criterion, our understanding can never fully qualify as knowledge.

Knowledge is not, however, entirely beyond our reach. We can make true statements about situations in which we do not participate, and even in understanding our own situation, we may approximate the truth to a greater or lesser extent. Nevertheless, there is bound to be some divergence between reality and our view of the world, and this divergence is itself part of reality. That is what renders reality so complicated. It will always exceed our complete comprehension. Reality is a moving target that remains just beyond our range forever. Participation and understanding interfere with each other, ensuring that our understanding is inherently imperfect and our actions have unintended consequences. I call the two-way connection between thinking and reality *reflexivity*, and it is the cornerstone of my conceptual framework.

RADICAL FALLIBILITY

Karl Popper, in his "Logic of Scientific Discovery" and other writings, argued that even scientific knowledge does not qualify as the ultimate truth. Scientific theories can never be verified; they are hypothetical in character, and even if supported by experiments, they should be accepted only as provisionally true because no amount of corroborating evidence can rule out the possibility that some contradictory evidence will turn up in the future. There is an asymmetry between verification and falsification that ensures that the ultimate truth remains permanently beyond our reach.

I regard the discovery of this asymmetry as Popper's greatest contribution to philosophy. It resolves the otherwise insoluble problem of induction: How can the fact that the sun has always risen in the east be used to prove that it will always do so? Popper's solution is to eliminate

the need for verification by declaring all scientific generalizations only provisionally valid, subject to falsification by
testing. Only testable generalizations qualify as scientific.

In my own work, I have taken Popper's conceptual
framework beyond the realm of scientific method. I applied it to social situations and formed a hypothesis that is
more radical than Popper's. Popper says that we may be
wrong; I contend that as participants, we are bound to be
wrong in some way or another, although the extent and
nature of our misunderstanding may vary. I call this *the
postulate of radical fallibility*.

Closely associated with the postulate is my concept of
fertile fallacies. We may start with a valid idea and, having
found it useful, extend it to areas to which it no longer
applies. For instance, natural science has produced impressive results, so we have applied its methods and criteria
to the study of social phenomena; yet the social situations
differ from natural phenomena insofar as social situations
have thinking participants who base their decisions on imperfect understanding. This renders a method that has
worked wonders in the study of nature somewhat misleading in the social field. It is in this sense that scientific
method can be considered a fertile fallacy.

Alternatively, the appeal of an idea may not depend on
its validity. For instance, primitive societies have endowed
inanimate objects with spirits and they attribute illnesses to
evil spirits. We know that these ideas are by scientific stan-

dards false, yet they obviously satisfy those who rely on them. The same applies to mythologies. Religions satisfy the believers but not the agnostics. The artistic imagination is fired by certain perceptions or forms of expression, but eventually the idea becomes exhausted. Often the deficiencies of a prevailing idea stimulate the emergence of another idea that may be considered its opposite. For instance, market fundamentalism has drawn its strength from the failures of socialism. I consider our entire civilization a product of fertile fallacies. I realize, of course, that this idea itself is, at best, a fertile fallacy.

Open Society

As participants in any given social situation, we must have some beliefs on which we base our actions. But on what basis can we act if we accept that our beliefs are likely to be false or incomplete renderings of reality? The answer is the same as the one Popper gave for the scientific method: We must treat our beliefs as provisionally true while keeping them open to constant reexamination. This is the foundation principle of an open society.

An open society holds itself open to improvement. It is based on the recognition that people have divergent views and interests and that nobody is in possession of the ultimate truth. Therefore, people must be given the greatest degree of freedom to pursue their interests as they see fit, provided that these interests can be reconciled with those of others. An open society needs institutions that allow people with divergent views and interests to live together in peace. Markets enable people to pursue their *private* interests through free exchange with others, but markets are not designed to take care of *common* interests such as the preservation of peace, the protection of the environment, or the maintenance of the market mechanism itself. Such common interests require political institutions, and it is here that the quandary of fallibility makes itself felt. Decisions must be made, but they are liable to be wrong; therefore, there must be a mechanism for correcting them. And, since perfection is unattainable, there must also be a mechanism for correcting the mechanism, ad infinitum.

The quandary has no resolution. Those who claim to have found an ultimate solution are bound to be wrong. They can impose their views only by repressing alternative views and by destroying what is so valuable in an open society: the freedom of thought, expression, and choice. Exactly where the limits of those freedoms are cannot be determined in the abstract; the limits must be decided by those who live in an open society. There is no single model of social organization to be followed.

THE HUMAN UNCERTAINTY PRINCIPLE

Fallibility affects not only our thinking but also the reality we are trying to understand. Fertile fallacies can go a long way in shaping the world in which we live. History revolved around religious heresies in the Middle Ages and the struggle between capitalism and communism during the Cold War. Many of the ideas and institutions we take for granted do not stand up to critical examination. Under the influence of natural science, we have come to think of reality as if it were well formed, in the sense that it obeys rules that are consistent with each other. That seems to hold true of natural phenomena, but not of situations that have thinking participants.

The radical fallibility of participants introduces an element of uncertainty into the situations in which they participate. I call this the *human uncertainty principle*. It is similar to the uncertainty principle in quantum physics, with an additional wrinkle: Heisenberg's discovery of the uncertainty principle—the impossibility of accurately measuring both an electron's position and its momentum at the same time—did not change the behavior of quantum particles one iota, but in the social sciences, the discovery or introduction of a new generalization can change the behavior of human participants. Marx's theory of history is the most obvious example and the one that Karl Popper had in sight when he wrote *Open Society and Its Enemies*. Marx sought to influence the course of history by claiming to predict it. But this is only one example of many. Mainstream economics, with its theory of the invisible hand, plays a similarly ambivalent role. On the one hand, it professes to be a scientific theory; on the other, it has been influential in shaping the global capitalist system as it currently prevails.* If the common interest is best served by people pursuing their self-interests, then it is in the common interest to liberate market participants from interference by the state or, worse still, by some international authority. That has been the guiding principle of globalization.

The ideology of American supremacy promoted by a dominant group within the Bush administration fits the same mold. In one of the most cogent expositions of the doctrine, the neoconservative Robert Kagan argues that there is a factual basis for the divergence between European and American attitudes toward the use of military power. Europe is weak; America is strong. Therefore, Europe is bound to favor international cooperation whereas America must follow a muscular foreign policy. As he puts it, "Americans are from Mars, Europeans from Venus."† It is noteworthy that Kagan and his intellectual fellow travelers use a neo-Marxist line of argument: The material con-

---

*Incidentally, Karl Marx's analysis of globalization in the *Communist Manifesto* published in 1848 makes interesting reading today. So does Karl Polanyi, *The Great Transformation* (Boston: Beacon Press, 1989).
†Robert Kagan, *Of Paradise and Power: America and Europe in the New World Order* (New York: Alfred A. Knopf, 2003).

ditions determine the ideological superstructure. Their goal is in fact similar to that pursued by Marx himself: They seek to influence policy and, to the extent they have succeeded, to justify it. It is remarkable how successful they have been. Marxism is out of favor, yet Kagan enjoys widespread acclaim in spite of the neo-Marxist roots of his reasoning and America is engaged in a futile and pernicious pursuit of supremacy clothed in a respectable-sounding argument.

Neo-Marxism, neoconservatism, and market fundamentalism all suffer from the same defect: They are rooted in nineteenth-century science, which took a deterministic view of the world. Charles Darwin maintained that the evolution of the species is determined by the struggle for survival. Karl Marx maintained that the ideological superstructure is determined by material conditions, that is to say, the prevailing ideology is determined by the prevailing class interests. Classical economists showed how the untrammeled pursuit of self-interest leads to an equilibrium that assures the optimal allocation of resources. It is the combination of these three ideas that has given rise to an ideology that combines a belief in markets with a belief in American supremacy: America has triumphed in the struggle for survival by giving market forces full play, and our success practically compels us to impose our views and interests on the world. But science has moved on since the nineteenth century.

Appendix

Modern science no longer takes a deterministic view of the universe. The survival of the fittest is not determined solely by competition; people's views are not determined solely by their material interests; and financial markets do not result in equilibrium. An ideology of American supremacy whose roots are in Darwin and Marx is both out of date and fallacious. It ignores the principle of human uncertainty and the postulate of radical fallibility, the guiding principles of an open society.

For the sake of completeness, I must point out that theories based on the human uncertainty principle are also bound to be flawed in one way or another; otherwise, they would invalidate the principle. Their inherent defect is that they do not yield determinate predictions. What brings them nevertheless closer to a true representation of reality than deterministic theories is that they refrain from making false claims and hold themselves open to modification in the light of experience. Open societies are more open to improvement than closed ones. My concept of fertile fallacies does not claim to be anything more than a fertile fallacy.

If our understanding is inherently flawed, the extent of our misunderstanding becomes all-important. This insight has led me to look at all sides of every argument. I am particularly sensitive to the deliberate distortions introduced by expressions such as "the war on terrorism" and "weapons of mass destruction"—not to mention more tendentious ones like "partial birth abortion" and the "death tax." But even when such manipulative distortions are successfully employed, there are bound to be unintentional divergences between outcomes and expectations. For instance, the invasion of Iraq was brought about through deliberate deception, but the results diverged significantly from those envisioned and intended by the campaign's planners.

The Alchemy of Finance

I have applied my basic insight concerning an inevitable divergence between reality and its interpretation to a better understanding of financial markets. Mainstream economics is built on the assumption that people know what is best for them; but as I have just explained, actors cannot base their decisions on true knowledge. Because the understanding on which they act is imperfect, their actions generate unintended consequences. Unintended consequences introduce an element of uncertainty into the course of events and make it difficult for economic theory to produce determinate predictions. Economists have sought to overcome this difficulty by claiming that markets as a whole know more than any individual participant; as a result, financial markets always tend toward equilibrium. The fluctuations that characterize financial markets can then be ascribed to so-called exogenous shocks or noise. But those concepts only serve to reconcile an unsound theory with reality.

The human uncertainty principle leads me to a different interpretation. Participants operate with a distorted view or bias and that bias goes into determining the prices that prevail in financial markets. But that is not all. Financial markets play an active role in determining the so-called fundamentals that they are supposed to reflect. There is two-way, reflexive interplay between reality and the participants' perceptions, which does not necessarily lead to equilibrium; in some cases, it may give rise to a boom-bust process. What distinguishes a boom-bust process or bubble from random fluctuations is that after a boom and bust, conditions do not return to the position from which they started. Instead of a timeless, eternal tendency toward equilibrium, financial markets are best understood as an endless historical process whose path is genuinely uncertain. I expounded this theory elsewhere; I shall briefly mention the various stages of a typical stock market bubble here because I find the pattern relevant to the Bush administration's pursuit of American supremacy.*

The process begins when a prevailing trend and a prevailing bias reinforce each other. As the bias becomes more pronounced, it becomes vulnerable to being corrected by the evidence. As long as the trend survives the

---

*The most up-to-date statement of my theory can be found in the new edition of my book *The Alchemy of Finance* (John Wiley & Sons, 2003).

test, it serves to reinforce the bias so that the bias can become quite far removed from reality. Eventually, there arrives a moment of truth, when participants become aware of the gap that separates their views from reality. A twilight period, when the trend is no longer reinforced by belief, ensues. In due course the trend is also reversed and a self-reinforcing process is set in motion in the opposite direction. Depending on how far a boom-bust process has carried, the reversal can be quite catastrophic, similar to a bubble's bursting.

Index

Index